A NEW OWNER'S
GUIDE TO
BULLDOGS

JG-139

Opposite page: The general appearance and attitude of the Bulldog should suggest great stability, vigor, and strength.

The Publisher wishes to acknowledge the following owners of the dogs in this book: Anna M. Benedetto, Theresa Campilango, Chuck and Mij Charbonneau, Chris and Sena Clark, Shirley Collier, Marlene Hall, Debra Ann Hogan, Mark and Deborah Jones, Professional Trainers Burt and Kim Lindemoen, Frieda McCullough, Pam Mattson, Dewey Ritter, Ray Spivey, Beverly Wagner, and Hank and Carol Williams.

Photographers: Isabelle Francais, Carl Lindemaier, Robert Pearcy, Vince Serbin, Robert Smith, Karen Taylor, and Jerry Vavra.

The author acknowledges the contribtion of Judy Iby of the following chapters: Sport of Purebred Dogs, Behavior and Canine Communication, Health Care, Identification and Finding the Lost Dog, and Traveling with Your Dog.

The Portrayal of canine pet products in this book is for general instructive value only; the appearance of such products does not necessarily constitute an endorsement by the authors, the publisher, or the owners of the dogs portrayed in this book.

Dedication

To all of our dogs who have enriched our lives beyond measure
"Qui me Amat, Amet et canem meum"

T.F.H. Publications, Inc.
One TFH Plaza
Third and Union Avenues
Neptune City, NJ 07753

This book has been published with the intent to provide accurate and authoritative information in regard to the subject matter within. While every precaution has been taken in preparation of this book, the publisher and author assume no responsibility for errors or omissions. Neither is any liability assumed for damages resulting from the use of the information herein.

ISBN 0-7938-2788-4

www.tfh.com

A New Owner's
Guide to
BULLDOGS

Carol & Henry Williams

Contents

2002 Edition

6 · History and Origin of the Bulldog
Birth of the Modern Bulldog · The Bulldog in America

16 · Characteristics of the Bulldog
Case for the Purebred Dog · Who Should Own a Bulldog? · Character of the Bulldog

Bulldog puppies grow up to look much like their parents.

28 · Standard of the Bulldog
An Overview of the Bulldog Standard

38 · Selecting the Right Bulldog for You
Recognizing a Healthy Puppy · Male or Female? · Selecting a Show-Prospect Puppy · Puppy or Adult · Important Papers · Health Guarantee · Temperament and Socialization · The Adolescent Bulldog

Well-cared-for and happy puppies are easy to pick out.

The Bulldog proves to have a very versatile personality that blends well with all types of family living.

58 · Caring for Your Bulldog
Feeding and Nutrition · Special Needs of the Bulldog · Illness and Injury · Bathing and Grooming

76 · Housebreaking and Training
Housebreaking · Basic Training · Leash Training · Training Classes · Versatility

96 · Sport of Purebred Dogs
Puppy Kindergarten · Conformation · Canine Good Citizen · Obedience · Tracking · Agility · General Information

110 · Behavior and Canine Communication
Canine Behavior · Socializing and Training · Understanding the Dog's Language · Body Language · Fear · Aggression · Problems

Your Bulldog's diet should include many nutritious foods and supplements.

126 · Health Care
The First Check up · The Physical Exam · Immunizations · Annual Visit · Intestinal Parasites · Other Internal Parasites · Heartworm Disease · External Parasites · To Breed or Not to Breed

142 · Dental Care for Your Dog's Life

148 · Identification and Finding the Lost Dog
Finding the Lost Dog

152 · Traveling with Your Dog
Trips · Air Travel · Boarding Kennels

Only the best will do for your Bulldog puppy, so do everything possible to safeguard him against all dangers.

HISTORY and Origin of the Bulldog

When you look at "Winston" lying on the sofa and perhaps snoring through his midday nap, it might seem impossible to imagine the Bulldog was ever anything other than the world's happiest couch potato. But when we begin to look into this breed's past we uncover a history of bravery, determination and alas, cruelty, that few dogs of any breed can equal. It is to this valiant breed's credit that he has not only survived the cruelty forced upon him but has become one of man's most friendly, docile and best-loved companions.

Of the countless breeds of dogs there is none more distinctive in appearance than today's Bulldog. Nor is there any other canine that has departed more drastically in appearance from his ancient ancestor *Canis lupis*, the wolf. The road from wolf-in-the-wild to Winston's noonday nap is long and fascinating.

How long it took for the wolf to move out of the forest and into man's cave dwellings is a point of conjecture. However, it seems obvious that observation of the wolf could easily have taught early man some effective hunting techniques that he too would be able to use advantageously. Also, many of the wolf's social habits might have seemed strikingly familiar to early man. The association grew from there.

The wolves that could assist in satisfying the unending human need for food were of course most highly prized. It also became

Of the countless breeds of dogs, there is no one more distinctive in appearance than today's Bulldog.

increasingly obvious as the man-wolf relationship developed through the ages, that certain descendants of these increasingly domesticated wolves could also be used by man to assist in survival pursuits other than hunting. Also highly valued were those wolves who were large enough and aggressive enough to protect man and the tribe he lived with from danger.

In their enlightening study of the development of dog breeds, *The Natural History of Dogs*, Richard and Alice Feinnes classify most

It is easy to see why the Bulldog is affectionately called the "sourmug."

dogs as having descended from one of four major groups: the Northern, the Dingo, the Greyhound and the Mastiff. Each of these groups trace back to separate and distinct branches of the wolf family.

The Arctic or Nordic group of dogs are direct descendants of the rugged northern wolf (*Canis lupis*). Included in the many breeds of this group are Alaskan Malamutes, Chows, German Shepherds and even the much smaller Welsh Corgis and Spitz type dogs.

The Dingo group traces its origin to the Asian wolf (*Canis lupis pallipes*). Two well known examples of the Dingo group are the Basenji and, through the admixture of several European breeds, the Rhodesian Ridgeback.

The Greyhound group descends from a coursing type relative of the Asian wolf and the group includes all those dogs that hunt

Despite his sometimes ferocious look, the Bulldog is one of the most docile, obedient, and trustworthy dogs one could ever own.

by sight and are capable of great speed. The Greyhound itself, the Afghan, the Borzoi and Irish Wolfhound are all examples of this group and are known as the coursing breeds.

The fourth classification, and that which we who study the origins of the Bulldog take special interest, is the Mastiff group which owes its primary heritage to the Tibetan wolf (*Canis lupis chanco* or *laniger*). The great diversity of dogs included in this group indicate they are not entirely of pure blood in that the specific breeds included have undoubtedly been influenced by descendants of the other three groups.

The breeds in this group, while comprised of a wide variation of types, do have a number of consistent characteristics. The ability to work by scent is typical. The heads of the dogs of the Mastiff group typically have pronounced stops and heads in which there is either a muzzle-skull length of proportionate size (mesaticephalic) or which have extremely short muzzles (brachycephalic). The ears of this group are pendant rather than pricked.

The tribes which occupied northern Europe were known to have kept large, fierce dogs of the Mastiff type. The Romans bred these Mastiff type dogs to fight in the arena against bulls, bears and other wild animals. The latter were known until the Middle Ages as Alains or Alaunts. In Britain these same large and fierce dogs became known as bandogs because ropes, chains or bands were employed to keep them under control.

The ferocious forerunners of today's Bulldog were brought about through manipulative breedings in England of these Alaunt or Mastiff type dogs. Their original purpose was to assist butchers in controlling the savage bulls from which food for the table would be gleaned. It was also believed that the meat of a much more tender and nutritious quality could be had from bulls which had been "worried" by these bandogs prior to butchering than that which came from bulls immediately slaughtered. The dogs were developed with short legs and heavy bodies that served them in keeping out of the way of the bulls' horns. It does not tax the imagination to see how readily what was a functional animal could rapidly be adapted to salve man's ego in cruel sport by pitting the dog against bull to see who owned the most ferocious

Bulldogs are the wonderful dogs they are because many dedicated breeders have spent years perfecting the breed.

dog most capable of bringing the bull to the ground. Thus was born the sport of "bull baiting."

In these contests, the dog was to grab the bull by the nose when the tethered bull attempted to impale the dog on its horns. The dog was to hold onto the bull with no regard to his own personal injury until the bull finally expired from loss of blood and oxygen deprivation.

The undershot jaw of the Bulldog enabled the dog to clamp onto the bull's nose with such a vice-like grip it was almost impossible for the bull to dislodge the dog. The dog's heavy body weight and low center of gravity combined with his sheer grit and determination could eventually bring the bull to ground.

It was from the duties assigned to these tenacious dogs that the characteristics that distinguish the Bulldog of today were developed. A head of great size provided the power required of the jaws to secure the iron grip on the bull's nose. The undershot and upward curving conformation of the muzzle (layback) not only provided as secure a hold as could be had, it also pushed the

The Bulldog's undershot jaw was so designed to enable him to clamp onto a bull's nose with a vice-like grip.

The Bulldog's wrinkles had the specific function of keeping the blood of a bull out of the dog's nose and eyes.

dog's nose back from the end of the muzzle so that even with jaws clamped tight, the dog's nose was free to take in needed air.

It goes without saying that this vice-like grip created a torrent of blood from the bull. Wrinkles of the dog's muzzle channeled this blood flow away from the dog's nose and eyes. So, the Bulldog's head, often dismissed simply as an anomaly, is in fact the result of form following function. Still, one is forced to wonder who else but the British stockmen of old could have conceived and developed the bizarre conformation of the Bulldog head as functional as it might have been?

Just prior to the close of the 1800s, the noted dog writer of that era, Hugh Dalziel, wrote: "When the rules of bull-baiting became consolidated, and the chief point was for the dog to run in farthest and fairest, tackling the bull in front, dogs would be selected and bred of low and strong formation. I think, unquestionable that we owe the present form of our Bulldog to the selection in breeding with the objects referred to made during the later period of bull-baiting, happily ending some 50 or 60 years ago."

Birth of the Modern Bulldog

An act of the English Parliament actually outlawed bull-baiting in 1835, but the practice was to take a good number of years until it was completely and finally ceased. When bull-baiting, bear-baiting and dog fighting were no longer practiced, Bulldog lovers turned to dog shows.

The first show at which a class for Bulldogs was offered was the Birmingham, England Kennel Club event held in 1860. Just a few years later in 1864 the first club organized specifically for "the perpetuation and the improvement of the old English Bulldog" was organized. The breed's first champion was King Dick owned by Jacob Lampier, one of the foremost breeder-exhibitors of the day.

Two of the most famous and influential Bulldogs of the time were "Rosa" and her mate, Ch. Sheffield Crib owned by H. Verelst. The painting of the famous pair by Abraham Coop is owned by The Kennel Club in England and hangs in the offices of that organization to this day.

At this time there was a great divergence in type. In fact, the divergence was so great it inspired a club member by the name of Wickens to write the landmark "Philo-Kuon Standard." While this standard of perfection was an important contribution to the breed, the club accomplished little else until the organization was reconstituted and revitalized in 1875.

The reorganized club produced a revised standard that in substance reflected the dictates of the Philo-Kuon Standard. The new standard however, omitted reference to Rosa, which had been described in the former standard as everything to be desired in a Bulldog.

By 1891 type had become a great controversy. It came to a head in the person of two dogs, both champions with impressive show records but of

Although bullbaiting was outlawed in 1835, the Bulldog has remained the same physically and has improved in temperament.

"Oliver" leaves no doubt that he owns the ground he stands on! He is owned by Pam Mattson.

widely divergent type. The show was the London Bulldog Society. The dogs were King Orry, a Bulldog of the old type—higher on leg, lighter in bone but very athletic with good head type and the other dog was Dockleaf, a smaller, low stationed dog of great bone that would not look out of place in today's competition.

The more modern Dockleaf was proclaimed winner of the show but the controversy did not end there. The owners of the two dogs fell into a heated discussion as to which dog was most physically able and a challenge, the famed "Bulldog Walk" came to pass.

The two dogs were to walk ten miles from Roe Buck at Lewisham to the Town Hall at Bromley for what was reputed to be "high stakes." Both set off gamely enough but Dockleaf fell by the wayside at two miles while King Orry finished the ten miles in great style.

In truth, the outcome was to decide which direction the breed should take—that of the past (King Orry) or of the future (Dockleaf).

Ironically the fanciers decided not upon the winner of the challenge but upon the future, Dockleaf. And thus was cast the form of today's Bulldog. The choice was made for form instead of function.

In an article wrote for England's *Dog World* newspaper, Mrs. Sheila Alcock, of the London Bulldog Society commented: "Debate this as we may, the modern Bulldog, with his faults and failings (and what breed is without them?) and his decisive totally recognizable 'Bulldogness,' would not have evolved without that decision of 1891."

THE BULLDOG IN AMERICA

The first known Bulldog to be shown in America was "Donald" owned and exhibited by Sir William Verner. Donald was shown in New York in 1880. The first Bulldog to become an American Kennel Club champion was the import Robinson Crusoe who achieved the title in 1888.

In April of 1890, H. D. Kendall called a meeting of interested Bulldog fanciers at Mechanics Hall in Boston, Massachusetts to discuss the best interests of the breed. It was unanimously decided

Although the breed no longer performs his task as bullbaiter, the Bulldog is still a dog of great stability, vigor, and strength.

to form an organization aimed at preserving the integrity of the breed. That organization continues on today as the Bulldog Club of America.

The BCA initially adopted the breed standard that was used by the Bulldog Club in England. However, just a few years later, American exhibitors felt that some clarifications were necessary and in 1894 adopted the revised standard that is basically the same standard used to this day.

According to the breed standard, the ideal Bulldog should be medium-sized, smooth-coated, with a heavy, thick-set, low-swung body.

The BCA has a unique system of regional clubs and specialty shows intended to preserve the integrity of the breed and give its membership as much direct participation as possible. The BCA was the first single-breed club admitted to the membership of the AKC.

While there have been many great winning Bulldogs through the years, only two have won the coveted Best in Show award at Westminster Kennel Club in New York. The first was an English import, Alex H. Stewart's Ch. Strathtay Prince Albert. Albert defeated all competition to reign supreme at Westminster in 1913. He was chosen for the Best in Show award by the English judge, Captain W. R. Beamish.

A long time, 42 years in fact, was to pass before another Bulldog would emerge victorious at Westminster. In 1955, Dr. John A. Saylor's American bred Ch. Kippax Fearnought was awarded Best in Show. The judge was Mr. Albert E. Van Court and Fearnought's handler was Harry Sangster.

CHARACTERISTICS of the Bulldog

If you are still in the "deciding" stage of whether or not you should bring a Bulldog puppy into your life, my advice is *do not*, I repeat do not visit a kennel or home in which there are Bulldog puppies. You will not leave without one! Wiggly, roly-poly, snub-nosed Bulldog puppies are absolutely irresistible. Of the many breeds we have known in our lifetimes, we find none so captivating as the baby Bulldog. The Bulldog's fans are loyal beyond description. What other dog fanciers have a special name for themselves in honor of their breed? Bulldoggers! Have you ever heard of a "Dobermaner" or a "Bichoner?"

It is for this very reason the person anticipating owning a Bulldog should give serious thought to the decision. Puppies are the material for millions of picture-postcards and greeting cards each year. Bulldog puppies are particularly used in this respect. There is nothing more seductive than a pile of Bulldog puppies, nestled together sound asleep, one on top of the other. But in addition to being cute, puppies are living, breathing and very mischievous little creatures and they are entirely dependent upon their human owner for *everything* once they leave their mother and littermates. This is particularly so of Bulldogs.

Buying any dog, especially a puppy, before someone is absolutely sure they want to make that commitment can be a serious mistake. The prospective dog owner must clearly understand the amount of time and work involved in dog ownership. Failure to

One must never forget Bulldog babies have an uncanny ability to squeeze themselves in and out of the most unimaginable places— especially the places they shouldn't be.

Robbie Benson is a well-known television and film star as well as movie director who fully appreciates the universal appeal of the Bulldog.

If you are unsure about purchasing a Bulldog, do not look at Bulldog puppies, because you will not be able to go home without one.

understand the extent of commitment dog ownership involves is one of the primary reasons there are so many unwanted canines that are forced to end their lives in an animal shelter.

Before anyone contemplates the purchase of a dog there are some very important conditions that must be considered. One of the first important questions that must be answered is whether or not the person who will ultimately be responsible for the dog's care and well being actually wants a dog.

All too often it is the mother of the household who must shoulder the responsibility of the family dog's day-to-day care. While the children in the family, perhaps even the father, may be wildly enthusiastic about having a dog, it must be remembered they are away most of the day at school or at work. It is often "mom" who will be taking on the additional responsibility of primary caregiver for the family dog.

Pets are a wonderful method of teaching children responsibility but it should be remembered that the enthusiasm which inspires children to promise anything in order to have a new puppy may quickly wane. Who will take care of the puppy once the novelty wears off? Does that person want a dog?

Desire to own a dog aside, does the lifestyle of the family actually provide for responsible dog ownership? If the entire family is away from home from early morning to late at night, who will provide for all of a puppy's needs? Feeding, exercise, outdoor access and the like cannot be provided if no one is home.

Another important factor to consider is whether or not the breed of dog is suitable for the person or the family with which it will be living. Some breeds can handle the rough and tumble play of young children. Some cannot. On the other hand some dogs are so large and clumsy, especially as puppies, that they could easily and unintentionally injure an infant.

Then too, there is the matter of hair. A luxuriously coated dog is certainly beautiful to behold but all that hair takes a great deal of care. At first thought, it would seem that a smooth-coated dog like the Bulldog would eliminate this problem. Not so, as we will see. While there is no long hair to contend with, there is a great deal the Bulldog owner is called upon to do in the way of skin care and cleanliness.

Chuck and Mij Charbonneau's "Budkis" is a man of the world and connoisseur of fine wines.

As great as claims are for any breed's intelligence and trainability, remember the new dog must be taught every household rule that it is to observe. Some dogs catch on more quickly than others and puppies are just as inclined to forget or disregard lessons as young children are.

CASE FOR THE PUREBRED DOG

As previously mentioned, all puppies are cute. Not all puppies grow up to be the picture of what we as humans find attractive. What is considered beauty by one person is not necessarily seen so by another. It is almost impossible to determine what a mixed breed puppy will look like as an adult. Nor will it be possible to determine if the mixed breed puppy's temperament is suitable for the person or family who wishes to own him. If the puppy grows up to be too big, too stubborn, or too active for the owner, what then will happen to him?

Size and temperament can vary to a degree even within a purebred breed. Still, selective breeding over many generations has produced dogs giving the would-be-owner reasonable assurance of what the purebred puppy will look and act like as an

Although Bulldog puppies appear to be almost identical, each develops his own personality, including likes and dislikes. A breeder can tell you much about the personality of each member of his litter.

Bulldogs have been among one of the favorite breeds of all time when it comes to selecting athletic team mascots.

adult. Points of attractiveness completely aside, this predictability is more important than one might think.

A person who wants a dog to go along on those morning jogs or long distance runs is not going to be particularly happy with a lethargic or short-legged breed like a Bulldog. Nor is the fastidious housekeeper, whose picture of the ideal dog is one which lies quietly at the feet of his master by the hour and never sheds, going to be particularly happy with the shaggy dog whose temperament is reminiscent of a hurricane.

Purebred puppies will grow up to look like their adult relatives and by and large they will behave pretty much like their the rest of their family. Any dog, mixed breed or not, has the potential to be a loving companion. However, a purebred dog offers reasonable assurance that it will not only suit the owner's lifestyle but the person's esthetic demands as well.

WHO SHOULD OWN A BULLDOG?

What kind of a person should own a Bulldog? As much as we love and cherish these dogs, they are not the dog for everyone.

There are many special considerations that must be taken into account before the decision to own a Bulldog is made. Through the years we have developed a list of special requirements for anyone who wishes to buy a Bulldog from us:

The dog must be a house dog 100% of the time: The Bulldog must be a "house dog!" He is not a breed that is able cope easily with temperature and humidity fluctuations. Nor is the breed able to endure being isolated from the people he loves. First and foremost the Bulldog is a people dog.

Yards must be completely fenced: Bulldogs are often described as being loyal and although our egos would have us believe that our dogs would pine away if they were not with us, this is hardly the truth. A Bulldog would be just as happy anywhere as long as he was fed, loved, petted and had a couch or chair to sleep on.

Bulldogs love people and they are not adverse to accepting an invitation to take a stroll with a passing child or hop into the car of a total stranger. For this reason the Bulldog owner must have a securely fenced yard.

No swimming pools: Most Bulldogs cannot swim but love the water. Even where pools have been completely fenced, there have been accidents when someone inadvertently left the gate open. It only takes a moment or two for a Bulldog to drown!

No home where a "macho" or aggressive dog is wanted: A home that encourages aggressive behavior is not the home for a Bulldog. A Bulldog in a fight is something you *never* want to see!

It is extremely important that the Bulldog owner knows how to keep his dog's exuberant nature in check. If a Bulldog pants too long and too hard, severe complications can arise.

Puppies follow bursts of activity with frequent "rest stops." Never allow your Bulldog puppy to play to exhaustion.

They become totally involved, their eyes glaze over and they are intent on doing great harm to whatever animal they are fighting with. Further, it is extremely dangerous for anyone, including the owner, to try and intervene as the Bulldog's complete and total concentration is on the fight and he has no sense of what he is biting!

No home where we haven't met everyone in the household: We want to meet everyone that our Bulldogs will be living with because it is important for us to see how each member will interact with the dog.

No home where only one of the adults is enthused about getting a Bulldog: Owning a Bulldog takes the cooperation of everyone in the household and Bulldogs have very special and often very limited appeal. No Bulldog is safe in an environment that it is not entirely receptive.

No home where children are responsible for the dog's care: We are very careful when we place a dog into a family with children. We want to make sure that the children will not be abusive to the dog since the dogs are very stoic and will take almost any abuse from a child. We want to protect our Bulldogs from that. At the same time, while the best of children can love and care for their dogs they are not always capable of understanding or remembering the very special care Bulldog ownership entails.

We had a call from a distraught family whose Bulldog had just died. They loved him so much they wanted to replace the dog immediately. When we asked the cause of death, we were told the following story.

It's not easy being a star! One of Kim Lindemoen's well-trained canine stars endures the pouring rain for her role in a made-for-TV film.

It was a warm (not hot) day. The children and the dog were outside playing. The children were called in to dinner but the dog was panting very hard so they left him outside to lie in the shade. When dinner was done and the children went back out to play, the dog was dead from heat prostration.

No home where they "want to get into breeding:" Breeding Bulldogs is extremely difficult on both dog and owner. It is not something to be attempted by most people. It takes a long time to understand what kind of stock is even suitable for breeding and an even longer time to learn the intricacies of breeding, whelping and rearing a litter of Bulldogs.

CHARACTER OF THE BULLDOG

A man may smile and bid you hail
yet wish you to the devil.
But when a Bulldog wags its tail
you know it's on the level!
Author unknown

The Bulldog is a docile, affectionate companion and yet will be playful and active (for short periods) if you want him to be. The breed is absolutely wonderful with children and the elderly. Their special talent in life is "companionship." Quite frankly we firmly believe that no breed has the talent for companionship to the degree that it is possessed by the Bulldog. A Bulldog may not give two hoots about guarding a missile site, but watch him take care of a toddler as the two amble along with the child holding steadfastly to the loose skin on the dog's throat.

When we are asked if Bulldogs make good watchdogs we always laughingly reply with: "Oh yes, they will gladly watch a burglar take everything in the house!" They will sometimes bark at strange noises (when and if they wake up!). Normally speaking Bulldogs do not bark much but you can hear them coming with their shuffling walk, their snorts of pleasure and, when they are asleep, their snores.

We once placed a Bulldog with a family that had a blind child. It worked out wonderfully because no matter where the dog was or what he was doing, the child could hear the dog and always find him. We get worried when we can't hear our Bulldogs!

However, in the Bulldog's favor are their forbidding looks. People who do not know the breed are usually terrified that the Bulldog temperament is as sour as the looks that gave the breed the nickname of "Sourmug." In most cases, this is as about as far from the truth as you can get. On the other hand, Bulldogs are brave to the extreme and will guard and defend their owner if they think their owner is being threatened.

When asked if Bulldogs make good watchdogs, the authors always reply, "Oh yes, they will gladly watch a burglar take everything in the house!"

Fighting

Not even the gentlest most docile Bulldog will back down from a fight with another dog if it is challenged. Hitting a Bulldog once engaged in a fight will do no good what so ever. The dog's mind is totally engaged in the fight and his body feels no pain. Forget yelling at the dog. Save your breath as a fighting Bulldog will not hear you. Avoid the situation ever occurring *at all costs*!

Bulldogs do not usually warn you with a growl before going for another dog. You will only get the signal if you are watching your dog and know what to look for. The signs are a slight stiffening of the body, intent eye contact with the other animal and his tongue will flick out rapidly a few times.

Immediately break your Bulldog's concentration if you observe these signs by turning his back to the other dog. Also be sure that when you do this the other dog is not going to get yours from behind! Remove your dog from the area at once.

It is important to remember that even though the situation may have developed only as far as described, your Bulldog will not forget it and if he builds up a grudge for a particular dog, it will be a lifelong problem. We cannot caution strongly enough to avoid allowing this to occur. If you notice your dog attempting to make that intense eye contact with another dog, stop it immediately by grabbing your dog by the jowls and say very sternly and forcefully, "No!" Then move to another area.

While Bulldogs can be tough with other dogs, their humans are their lives. They are clowns and will do things just to make you laugh. They are also very sensitive to your moods and will sympathize with you, rejoice with you and be still or grieve with you.

"Gabe" owned by Pam Mattson. Part of the charm of the Bulldog is that they look so tough but aren't at all. Bulldogs are gentle and dignified.

Bulldogs are gentle and dignified. Part of their charm is that they look so tough but they aren't at all. Their inner beauty will steal your heart. When it comes to their humans, Bulldogs are totally forgiving and totally loving. They are true companions in every sense of the word.

Grown-up Bulldogs can develop a fondness for toddlers, both human and canine, that extends to a willingness to risk their lives.

STANDARD of the Bulldog

General Appearance—The perfect Bulldog must be of medium size and smooth coat; with heavy, thickset, low-swung body, massive short-faced head, wide shoulders and sturdy limbs. The general appearance and attitude should suggest great stability, vigor and strength. The disposition should be equable and kind, resolute and courageous (not vicious or aggressive), and demeanor should be pacific and dignified. These attributes should be countenanced by the expression and behavior.

Size, Proportion, Symmetry—The size for mature dogs is about 50 pounds; for mature bitches about 40 pounds. *Proportion*—The circumference of the skull in front of the ears should measure at least the height of the dog at the shoulders.

The Bulldog's forelegs are short, very stout, straight, and muscular. Set wide apart, they should be present in a bowed outline.

Symmetry—The "points" should be well distributed and bear good relation one to the other, no feature being in such prominence from either excess or lack of quality that the animal appears deformed or ill-proportioned. *Influence of Sex*— In comparison of specimens of different sex, due allowance should be made in favor of the bitches, which do not bear the characteristics of the breed to the same degree of perfection and grandeur as do the dogs.

Ears should be small, thin, and set high on the head. They should never be cropped or carried erect.

Head—*Eyes and Eyelids*—The eyes, seen from the front, should be situated low down in the skull, as far from the ears as possible, and their corners should be in a straight line at right angles with the stop. They should be quite in front of the head, as wide apart as possible, provided their outer corners are within the outline of the cheeks when viewed from the front. They should be quite round in form, of moderate size, neither sunken nor bulging, and in color should be very dark. The lids should cover the white of the eyeball, when the dog is looking directly forward, and the lid should show no "haw." *Ears*—The ears should be set high in the head, the front inner edge of each ear joining the outline of the skull at the top back corner of skull, so as to place them as wide apart, and as high, and as far from the eyes as possible. In size they should be small and thin. The shape termed "rose ear" is the most desirable. The rose ear folds inward at its back lower edge, the upper front edge curving over, outward and backward, showing part of the inside of the burr. (The ears should not be carried erect or prick-eared or buttoned and should never be cropped.) *Skull*— The skull should be very large, and in circumference, in front of the ears, should measure at least the height of the dog at the shoulders. Viewed from the front, it should appear very high from the corner of the lower jaw to the apex of the skull, and also very broad and square. Viewed at the side, the head

A Bulldog puppy will grow to look much like his parents so be certain they are good specimens of the breed.

should appear very high, and very short from the point of the nose to occiput. The forehead should be flat (not rounded or domed), neither too prominent nor overhanging the face. *Cheeks*—The cheeks should be well rounded, protruding sideways and outward beyond the eyes. *Stop*—The temples or frontal bones should be very well defined, broad, square and high, causing a hollow or groove between the eyes. This indentation, or stop, should be both broad and deep and extend up the middle of the forehead, dividing the head vertically, being traceable to the top of the skull. *Face and Muzzle*—The face, measured from the front of the cheekbone to the tip of the nose, should be extremely short, the muzzle being very short, broad, turned upward and very deep from the corner of the eye to the corner of the mouth. *Nose*—The nose should be large, broad and black, its tip set back deeply between the eyes. The distance from bottom of stop, between the eyes, to the tip of nose should be as short as possible and not exceed the length from the tip of nose to the edge of underlip. The nostrils should be wide, large and black, with a well-defined line between them. Any nose other than black is objectionable and a brown or liver-colored nose shall *disqualify*. *Lips*—The chops or "flews" should be thick, broad, pendant and very deep, completely overhanging the lower jaw at each side. They join the underlip in front and almost or quite cover the teeth, which should be scarcely noticeable when the mouth is closed. *Bite—Jaws*—The jaws should be massive, very broad, square and "undershot," the lower jaw projecting considerably in front of the upper jaw and turning up. *Teeth*—The teeth should be large and strong, with the canine teeth or tusks wide

The Bulldog's shoulders should be muscular and his chest should be broad.

apart, and the six small teeth in front, between the canines, in an even, level row.

Neck, Topline, Body—*Neck*—The neck should be short, very thick, deep and strong and well arched at the back. *Topline*—There should be a slight fall in the back, close behind the shoulders (its lowest part), whence the spine should rise to the loins (the top of which should be higher than the top of the shoulders), thence curving again more suddenly to the tail, forming an arch (a very distinctive feature of the breed), termed "roach back" or, more correctly, "wheel-back." *Body*—

Ch. Fairwood's Lil' Beauregard shows us just what the standard has to say about the Bulldog's short, broad, and upturned muzzle.

The brisket and body should be very capacious, with full sides, well-rounded ribs and very deep from the shoulders down to its lowest part, where it joins the chest. It should be well let down between the shoulders and forelegs, giving the dog a broad, low, short-legged appearance. *Chest*—The chest should be very broad, deep and full. *Underline*—The body should be well ribbed up behind with the belly tucked up and not rotund. *Back and Loin*—The back should be short and strong, very broad at the shoulders and comparatively narrow at the loins. *Tail*—The tail may be either straight or "screwed" (but never curved or curly), and in any case must be short, hung low, with decided downward carriage, thick root and fine tip. If straight, the tail should be cylindrical and of uniform taper. If "screwed," the bends or kinks should be well defined, and they may be abrupt and even knotty, but no portion of the member should be elevated above the base or root.

Forequarters—*Shoulders*—The shoulders should be muscular, very heavy, widespread and slanting outward, giving stability and

Author Henry J. "Hank" Williams is pictured winning the Non-Sporting Group with his owner-handled Ch. Aanneglenn's Make My Day.

Your Bulldog will do his best to understand everything you say so keep it simple and be consistent.

great power. *Forelegs*—The forelegs should be short, very stout, straight and muscular, set wide apart, with well developed calves, presenting a bowed outline, but the bones of the legs should not be curved or bandy, nor the feet brought too close together. *Elbows*—The elbows should be low and stand well out and loose from the body. *Feet*—The feet should be moderate in size, compact and firmly set. Toes compact, well split up, with high knuckles and very short stubby nails. The front feet may be straight or slightly out-turned.

Hindquarters—*Legs*—The hind legs should be strong and muscular and longer than the forelegs, so as to elevate the loins above the shoulders. Hocks should be slightly bent and well let down, so as to give length and strength from the loins to hock. The lower leg should be short, straight and strong, with the stifles turned slightly outward and away from the body. The hocks are thereby made to approach each other, and the hind feet to turn outward. *Feet*—The feet should be moderate in size, compact and firmly set. Toes compact, well split up, with high knuckles and short stubby nails. The hind feet should be pointed well outward.

Coat and Skin—*Coat*—The coat should be straight, short, flat, close, of fine texture, smooth and glossy. (No fringe, feather or curl.) *Skin*—The skin should be soft and loose, especially at the head, neck and shoulders. *Wrinkles and Dewlap*—The head and face should be covered with heavy wrinkles, and at the throat, from jaw to chest, there should be two loose pendulous folds, forming the dewlap.

Color of Coat—The color of coat should be uniform, pure of its kind and brilliant. The various colors found in the breed are to be preferred in the following order: (1) red brindle, (2) all other brindles, (3) solid white, (4) solid red, fawn or fallow, (5) piebald, (6) inferior qualities of all the foregoing. Note: A perfect piebald is preferable to a muddy brindle or defective solid color. Solid black is very undesirable, but not so objectionable if occurring to a moderate degree in piebald patches. The brindles to be perfect should have a fine, even and equal distribution of the composite colors. In brindles and solid colors a small white patch on the chest is not considered detrimental. In piebalds the color patches should be well defined, of pure color and symmetrically distributed.

Gait—The style and carriage are peculiar, his gait being a loose-jointed, shuffling, sidewise motion, giving the characteristic "roll." The action must, however, be unrestrained, free and vigorous.

Temperament—The disposition should be equable and kind, resolute and courageous (not vicious or aggressive), and demeanor should be pacific and dignified. These attributes should be countenanced by the expression and behavior.

Your Bulldog's gait is a loose-jointed shuffling, sidewise motion, giving the characteristic "roll." The action must, however, be unrestrained, free and vigorous.

Scale of Points
General Properties
Proportion and Symmetry. 5
Attitude 3
Expression 2
Gait 3
Size 3
Coat 2
Color of Coat 4

                        22

Head
Skull 5
Cheeks 2
Stop 4
Eyes and Eyelids 3
Ears 5
Wrinkle 5
Nose 6
Chops 2
Jaws 5
Teeth 2

                        39

Body, Legs, etc.
Neck 3
Dewlap 2
Shoulders 5
Chest 3
Ribs 3
Brisket 2
Belly 2
Back 5
Forelegs and Elbows 4
Hind Legs 3
Feet 3
Tail 4

                        39

Total.........100

DISQUALIFICATION
Brown or liver-colored nose.
Approved July 20, 1976
Reformatted November 28, 1990

AN OVERVIEW OF THE BULLDOG STANDARD

The AKC standard of the Bulldog is written in simple straightforward language that can be read and understood by even the beginning fancier. However, its implications take many years to fully understand. This can only be accomplished through observing many quality Bulldogs over the years and reading as much about the breed as possible. A good many books have been written about the breed and it is well worth the Bulldog owner's time and effort to digest their contents if he or she is interested in showing or breeding this breed.

There are some breeds which change drastically from puppyhood to adulthood. It would be extremely difficult for the untrained eye to determine the actual breed of some purebred dogs in puppyhood. This is not so with the Bulldog. Most are inclined to agree that in many respects a six-week-old Bulldog puppy will reflect in miniature what it will look at maturity.

It must be remembered that the breed standard describes the "perfect" Bulldog, and that no dog is perfect, and no Bulldog, not even the greatest dog show winner, will possess every quality asked for in its perfect form. It is how closely an individual dog adheres to the standard of the breed that determines its show potential.

Above all, a Bulldog should convey an appearance of strength and vigor. One without the other makes the Bulldog useless. It lacks breed type. The Bulldog standard asks for a dog that is sound in both body and temperament.

While the standard takes great pains to describe in detail all that is desirable in the breed, in the end the reader should come away with the picture of a dog that owns the ground it stands upon; sound of both limb and mind. Never too small, nor too big. It is a medium-sized dog and the opposite ends of the size spectrum do not conjure up a dog that is at once both strong and vigorous.

In conformation shows, the dogs are evaluated on how close they come to the standard, or ideal, for the breed.

Note the characteristic rose ear of the Bulldog, which folds inward at its back lower edge. The upper front edge curves over and backward, revealing part of the inside burr.

The look of the Bulldog both in body and expression underscores its character—kind, courageous and dignified. That is the essence of the Bulldog temperament.

Proportion, balance and symmetry are key in assessing Bulldog quality. The parts "fit." A head too large or a body too small would never give the total picture of what the standard conveys. Look at the dog in profile. The line of the balanced dog seems to flow from the tip of the Bulldog's chin to the end of its tail.

Many breed experts consider the head of a breed is that characteristic which distinguishes it from all others. In no case is this more true than with the Bulldog. The expression of the Bulldog is captured in its affectionate moniker, "Sourmug." The shape of the head is most often referred to as brick shaped. Unique in every respect, the Bulldog head requires a great deal of study before it is fully understood.

Movement too is Bulldog distinctive. The Bulldog moves with what is referred to as a "roll." The breed's wide front construction combined with its much narrower rear result in an ambling movement that helps characterize that solid, surefooted character so important to the Bulldog.

SELECTING the Right Bulldog for You

The Bulldog puppy you bring into your home will be your best friend and a member of your family for many years to come. The average well-bred and well cared for Bulldog lives to be about 8 years old. Having said that, we presently have a healthy 10-year-old bitch and have known others to live to be 13. The Bulldog longevity record is undoubtedly owned by a dog named Samuel Ellsworth who was owned by Mark and Deborah Jones. Samuel attended the 1994 Bulldog Club of America National Specialty at the age of 17 and lived on to the following year as well!

Early care and sound breeding is vital to the longevity of your Bulldog. Therefore it is of the utmost importance that the dog you select has had every opportunity to begin life in a healthy, stable environment and comes from stock that is both physically and temperamentally sound.

The only way you can be assured of this is to go directly to a breeder of Bulldogs who has consistently produced dogs of this kind over the years. A breeder earns this reputation through a well-planned breeding program that has been governed by rigid selectivity. Selective breeding programs are aimed at maintaining the breed's many fine qualities and keeping the breed free of as many genetic weaknesses as possible.

"Bo" and "Annie," lifelong pals bred and owned by Pam Mattson.

Anyone who has ever bred dogs will quickly tell you this selective process is both time consuming and costly for a breeder and that no one ever makes money breeding sound and healthy dogs. One of the many things it does accomplish, however, is to ensure you of getting a

If there is a show career in your puppy's future, it is never too soon to begin ring training. Holding the future show dog in a show pose for just a minute or so accustoms it to more demanding training when it reaches adulthood.

Bulldog that will be a joy to own. Responsible Bulldog breeders protect their tremendous investment of time and money by basing their breeding programs on the healthiest most representative breeding stock available. These breeders provide each following generation with the very best care, sanitation and nutrition available.

Governing kennel clubs in the different countries of the world maintain lists of local breed clubs and breeders that can lead a prospective Bulldog buyer to responsible breeders of quality stock. If you are not sure of where to contact an established Bulldog breeder in your area, we strongly recommend contacting your kennel club for recommendations.

There is little doubt that you will be able to find an established Bulldog breeder in your own area. Finding a local breeder will allow you to visit the breeder's home or kennel, inspect the facility and in many cases you will also be able to see a puppy's parents and other relatives. Good breeders are always willing and able to discuss any problems that might exist in the breed and how they should be dealt with.

The trouble with misbehaving Bulldog puppies is that they are always convinced they are completely innocent.

If there aren't any Bulldog breeders in your immediate area, rest assured taking the time and exerting the effort to plan a trip to a reputable breeder will be well worth your while. Shipping Bulldogs by air, whether they are puppies or adults, is a risky business at best and many Bulldog breeders simply will not do so.

Never hesitate to ask the breeder you visit or speak to on the phone any questions or concerns you might have relative to Bulldog ownership. We ask many questions of those who anticipate purchasing a Bulldog from us. Expect any Bulldog breeder to ask these and perhaps even more questions as well. Good breeders are just as interested in placing their Bulldog puppies in a loving and safe environment as you are in obtaining a happy, healthy puppy.

Not all good breeders maintain large kennels. In fact, you are more apt to find Bulldogs come from the homes of small-hobby breeders who keep only a few dogs and have litters only occasionally. The names of these people are just as likely to appear on the recommended lists from kennel clubs as the larger kennels that maintain many dogs. Hobby breeders are equally dedicated to breeding quality Bulldogs. A factor in favor of the hobby breeder is his distinct advantage of being able to raise puppies in the home environment with the all the accompanying personal attention and socialization.

Again, it is important that both the buyer and the seller ask questions. Be extremely suspicious of anyone who is willing to sell you a Bulldog puppy with no questions asked.

Recognizing a Healthy Puppy

Bulldog breeders seldom release their puppies until the puppies are at least eight weeks of age and have been given their first and perhaps second set of puppy inoculations. By the time the litter is eight weeks of age they are entirely weaned. While puppies are nursing they have complete immunity to disease. Once they have stopped nursing, however, they become highly susceptible to many infectious diseases. A number of these diseases can be transmitted on the hands and clothing of humans. Therefore, it is extremely important that your puppy is current on all the shots he must have for his age.

A healthy Bulldog puppy is a bouncy, playful extrovert. Bulldog puppies are not phlegmatic! His attitude should be happy and friendly. Personalities and temperaments within a litter can range from very active to completely passive. Some puppies are ready to play with the world, others simply want to crawl up into your lap and be held. While you never select a puppy that appears shy or listless because you feel sorry for him, we would not hesitate to select the puppy that is quiet and reserved just as long as he is healthy.

Taking a puppy that appears sickly and needy will undoubtedly lead to heartache and expensive veterinary costs. Do not attempt to make up for what the breeder did not do in providing proper care and nutrition. It seldom works.

If you select one of the very active puppies, you must be sure that you have the extreme patience that will be needed to train him. This type of puppy may be very intelligent but demanding and contrary. Like precocious children, this type of Bulldog likes to have his own way. You must be prepared to meet this very challenging personality with patience, firmness, love and consistency. We can not stress the word consistency enough!

If at all possible take the Bulldog puppy you are attracted to into a different room in the kennel or house in which he was raised. The smells will remain the same for the puppy so he should still feel secure but it will give you an opportunity to see how the puppy acts away from his littermates and it will give you an opportunity to inspect the puppy more closely.

Above all, the puppy should be clean. The skin should be pliable and the coat soft. A healthy puppy's ears will be pink and clean. Dark discharge or a bad odor could indicate ear mites—a sure sign of lack of cleanliness and poor maintenance. A Bulldog puppy's breath should always smell sweet. The nose of the healthy puppy is cold and wet and there should be no discharge of any kind.

Check the wrinkles and the tail (top and bottom). Those areas should be dry and clean. There should be no sores or excess moisture. Check the top of the head for any malformation. There should never be any malformation of the jaw, lips or nostrils. Make sure there is no rupture of the navel.

The puppy's teeth must be clean and bright and his eyes should be dark and clear. Runny eyes or eyes that appear red and irritated could be caused by a myriad of problems, none of which indicate a healthy puppy. Coughing or diarrhea are absolute danger signals.

While Bulldog puppies cannot be accused of being the epitome of style and grace, their movement should still be free and easy

When selecting a healthy Bulldog, look for one that is alert, curious, and interested in his surroundings. He should be active and playful.

and they should never express any difficulty in moving about. Sound conformation can be determined even at eight or ten weeks of age.

The puppy's attitude tells you a great deal about his state of health. Puppies which are feeling "out of sorts" react very quickly and will usually find a warm littermate to snuggle up to and prefer to stay that way even when the rest of the "gang" wants to play or go exploring.

MALE OR FEMALE?

The sex of a dog in many breeds is an important consideration and of course there are sex related differences in the Bulldog that the prospective buyer should consider. In the end, however, the assets and liabilities of each sex do balance each other out and the final choice remains with individual preference.

The male Bulldog simply has more of everything—more size, more weight, more aggressiveness (particularly around other males!) and more to care for. However, in the end, the male Bulldog makes just as loving, devoted and trainable companion as the female. He can of course be a bit more headstrong as an adolescent, and this will require a bit more patience on the part of his owner. Here again, the owner's dedication to establishing and maintaining discipline will determine the final outcome.

Females have their semiannual "heat" cycles once they have reached sexual maturity. These cycles usually occur for the first time at about nine or ten months of age are accompanied by a bloody vaginal discharge. The discharge creates the need to confine the female so that she does not soil her surroundings. It must be understood that the female has no control over this bloody discharge so it has nothing to do with training.

Confinement of the female in heat is especially important to prevent unwanted attention from some neighborhood Lothario. While it may be difficult to get a female Bulldog bred under normal circumstances, if any dog is going to be able to do it, it will be the one you most definitely do not want her bred to!

Both of the sexually related problems can be eliminated by spaying the female and neutering the male. Unless a Bulldog is purchased expressly for breeding or showing from a breeder capable of making this judgment, your pet should be sexually altered.

Breeding and raising Bulldogs should be left in the hands of people who have the facilities and knowledge to do the job properly. Only those who have the facilities to keep each and every puppy they breed until the correct home is found for it should ever contemplate raising a litter. This can often take many months after a litter is born. Most single dog owners are not equipped to do this.

Though Bulldog puppies are stocky little guys, they should never feel bloated or spongy. These two pups owned by Mark and Deborah Jones are excellent examples of what well-cared-for puppies should look like.

Pam Mattson's "Hannah" reflects on the "Summer of '92." Your Bulldog will be with you for a great many years, so treat her with great love and respect each day of her life.

Naturally, a responsible dog owner would never allow his or her pet to roam the streets and end his life in an animal shelter. Unfortunately, being forced to place a puppy due to space constraints before you are able to thoroughly check out the prospective buyer may in fact create this exact situation.

Parents will often ask to buy a female "just as a pet" but with full intentions of breeding so that their children can witness "the miracle of birth." There are countless books and videos now available which portray this wonderful event. Altering one's companion dog eliminates bothersome household problems and precautions.

In the case of adult dogs we place in homes, we always have them altered first. This way the dogs do not have to go through surgery while they are adjusting to their new homes. With the advent of early spaying and neutering, it is now also possible to have puppies altered as early as 12 weeks of age. Responsible breeders have the surgery done before placing their pet puppies.

It should be understood however, that spaying and neutering are not reversible procedures. Spayed females or neutered males are not allowed to be shown in the conformation shows of most countries, nor will altered animals ever be able to be used for breeding.

SELECTING A SHOW-PROSPECT PUPPY

If you or your family are considering a show career for your puppy we strongly advise putting yourself in the hands of an established breeder who has earned a reputation for breeding winning show dogs. They and they alone are most capable of anticipating what one might expect a young puppy of their line to develop into when he reaches maturity.

Although the potential buyer should read the official breed standard for the Bulldog, it is hard for the novice to really understand the nuances of what is being asked. The experienced breeder is best equipped to do so and will be only too happy to assist you in your quest. Even at that, no one can make accurate predictions or guarantees on a very young puppy.

Any predictions a breeder is apt to make are based upon the breeder's experience with past litters that produced winning show dogs. It should be obvious that the more successful a

Bulldogs are gentle and make great companions for children. Make sure children understand that a puppy is not a toy and must be handled with love and respect.

Art can take some very curious forms. Who can deny creating the Bulldog was not art indeed?

breeder has been in producing winning Bulldogs through the years, the broader his or her basis of comparison will be.

The most any responsible breeder will say about an eight-week-old puppy is that it has "show potential." If you are serious about showing your Bulldog, most breeders strongly suggest waiting until a puppy is at least four or five months old before making any decisions.

There are many "beauty point" shortcomings a Bulldog puppy might have that would in no way interfere with it being a wonderful companion. At the same time these faults could be serious drawbacks in the show ring. Many of these faults are such that a beginner in the breed might hardly notice. This is why employing the assistance of a good breeder is so important. Still, the prospective buyer should be at least generally aware of what the Bulldog show puppy should look like and know what faults constitute "disqualifications" that would bar a Bulldog from being shown in conformation shows.

All of the foregoing regarding soundness and health in selecting a companion puppy apply to the show puppy as well. The show prospect must be sound, healthy and adhere to the standard of the breed very closely.

The more you know about the history and development of the breed, the better equipped you will be to see the differences that distinguish the show dog from the pet.

The things that really define a show prospect puppy are type, balance and temperament. Three simple words that have so many nuances it takes most breeders an entire lifetime to fully comprehend even a good part of them.

Type: Type includes the characteristics that truly typify the breed. Paramount among these features of course is the Bulldog's head with the large skull and face that is broad and wrinkled. The ears must be small and thin in order to achieve the "rosed" look as an adult. The nose should be large and black, set way back almost between the eyes and there should be a deep stop between the eyes. Look for a broad underjaw with teeth in a straight line.

Another important and distinguishing feature of the Bulldog is his "roached" back. This is a moderately curved, rather than flat, back line. The body is short and pear-shaped looking from above. That is, it is much wider at the shoulder than it is at the hips.

The bones of the puppy's forelegs should be strong and straight and the feet are tight and compact. The legs should be short. The puppy may have a perfectly straight or a screw tail. Either is quite correct.

Balance: Balance is the manner in which all the desirable characteristics fit together. Their combination creates the picture of quality that says, "I am the best Bulldog that ever was!"

Temperament: The correct Bulldog temperament combines all those wonderful characteristics we have been discussing thus far. In the show ring the Bulldog is a solid performer who makes it obvious he owns every inch of the ground he stands on.

Puppy or Adult?

For the person anticipating a show career for their Bulldog or for someone hoping to become a breeder, the purchase of a young adult provides greater certainty with respect to quality. Even those who simply want a companion should consider the adult dog.

In some instances breeders will have males or females they no longer wish to use for breeding and after the dogs have been altered would prefer to have them live out their lives in a private home with all its attendant care and attention. Acquiring an adult dog eliminates the many problems raising

Even grown-up Bulldogs can take a notion to "redecorate" your home. Avoid accidents by making sure your Bulldog and your valuables are in a safe place when you leave home.

a puppy involves and Bulldogs are a breed that can "transfer" well provided they are given the affection and attention they need.

Elderly people often prefer the adult dog, particularly one that is housebroken. The adult dog can be easier to manage, requiring less supervision and damage control. Adult Bulldogs are seldom "chewers" and are usually more than ready to adapt to household rules.

There are things to consider though. Adult dogs have usually developed behaviors that may or may not fit into your routine. If an adult Bulldog has never been exposed to small children the dog may be totally perplexed, often frightened, by this new experience. Children are also inclined to be more active and vocal than the average adult and this could intimidate the dog as well.

Then too, there is the problem of other pets. A Bulldog that has never been around other animals, particularly cats, will probably have an extremely difficult if not impossible task of adjusting to them.

We strongly advise taking an adult Bulldog on a trial basis to see if the dog will adapt to the new owner's lifestyle and environment. Most often it works but on rare occasions a prospective owner decides training his or her dog from puppyhood is worth the time and effort required.

IMPORTANT PAPERS

The purchase of any purebred dog entitles you to four very important documents: a health record which includes a list of inoculations, a copy of the dog's pedigree, a registration certificate and the dog's diet sheet.

Health and Inoculation Records: You will find that most Bulldog breeders have initiated the necessary preliminary inoculation series for their puppies by the time they are eight weeks of age. These inoculations temporarily protect the puppies against hepatitis, leptospirosis, distemper and canine parvovirus. "Permanent" inoculations will follow at a prescribed time. Since breeders and veterinarians follow different approaches to inoculations it is important that the health record you obtain for your puppy accurately lists which shots have been given and when. In this way the veterinarian you choose will be able to continue on with the appropriate inocul-ation series as needed. In most cases rabies inoculations are not given until a puppy is six months of age or older.

When you acquire your new Bulldog puppy you will be given a number of papers from the breeder such as a health record with all shots listed that your puppy received, your dog's pedigree, registration certificate and diet sheet.

Pedigree: The pedigree is your dog's "family tree." The breeder must supply you with a copy of this document authenticating your puppy's ancestors back to at least the third generation. All purebred dogs have pedigrees. The pedigree in itself does not mean that your puppy is of show quality. All it means is that all of his ancestors were in fact registered Bulldogs. They may all have been of pet quality.

Unscrupulous puppy dealers often try to imply that a pedigree indicates that all dogs having one are of championship caliber. This is not true. Again, it simply tells you all of the dog's ancestors are purebred.

Registration certificate: A registration certificate is the canine world's "birth certificate." This certificate is issued by a country's

They call it puppy love—and Bulldog puppies are ready to share this with man and beast.

governing kennel club. When the ownership of your Bulldog is transferred from the breeder's name to your name, the transaction is entered on this certificate and once mailed to the appropriate kennel club, it is permanently recorded in their computerized files.

Keep all of your dog's documents in a safe place as you will need them when you visit your veterinarian or should you ever wish to breed or show your Bulldog. Keep the name, address and phone number of the breeder from whom you purchase your dog in a separate place as well. Should you ever lose any of these important documents, you will then be able to contact the breeder regarding obtaining duplicates.

Diet Sheet: Your Bulldog is the happy healthy puppy he is because the breeder has been carefully feeding and caring for him. Every breeder we know has their own particular way of doing this. Most breeders give the new owner a written record that details the amount and kind of food a puppy has been receiving. Do follow these recommendations to the letter at least for the first month or two after the puppy comes to live with you.

The diet sheet should indicate the kinds of food and number of times a day your puppy has been accustomed to being fed. The kinds of vitamin supplementation the puppy has been receiving is also important. Following the prescribed procedure will reduce the chance of upset stomach and loose stools.

Usually a breeder's diet sheet projects the increases and changes in food that will be necessary as your puppy grows from week to week. If the sheet does not include this information ask the breeder for suggestions regarding increases and the eventual change over to adult food.

In the unlikely event you are not supplied with a diet sheet by the breeder and are unable to get one, your veterinarian will be able to advise you in this respect. There are countless foods now being manufactured expressly to meet the nutritional needs of puppies and growing dogs. A trip down the pet aisle at your super market will prove just how many choices there are. Two important tips to remember: read labels carefully for content and when dealing with established, reliable manufacturers you are more likely to get what you pay for.

This curious onlooker seems hard pressed to believe "those little things" are really Bulldogs.

HEALTH GUARANTEE

Any reputable breeder is more than willing to supply a written agreement that the purchase of your Bulldog is contingent upon its passing a veterinarian's examination. Ideally you will be able to arrange an appointment with your chosen veterinarian right after you have picked up your puppy from the breeder and before you take the puppy home. If this is not possible you should not delay this

A well-socialized Bulldog puppy will get along with dogs as well as humans.

procedure any longer than 24 hours from the time you take your puppy home.

TEMPERAMENT AND SOCIALIZATION

Temperament is both hereditary and learned. Inherited good temperament can be ruined by poor treatment and lack of proper socialization. A Bulldog puppy that comes from shy or nervous stock or stock that is uncontrollably aggressive is a poor risk as either a companion or show dog and should certainly never be bred from. Therefore, it is critical that you obtain a happy puppy from a breeder who is determined to produce good temperaments and has taken all the necessary steps early on to provide the early socialization necessary.

Taking your puppy to "puppy kindergarten" class is one of the best things you can do for it. There he will learn basic household manners as well as how to interact with other dogs and people. He absolutely must learn to walk on a leash at your side without pulling.

Temperaments in the same litter can range from confident and outgoing on the high end of the scale to shy and fearful at the low end but by and large the Bulldog temperament is and should be confident and friendly.

If you are fortunate enough to have children in the household or living nearby, your socialization task will be assisted considerably. Bulldogs raised with well supervised children are the best. The two seem to understand each other and in some way known only to the puppies and children themselves, they give each other the confidence to face the trying ordeal of growing up.

The children in your own household are not the only children your puppy should spend time with. It is a case of the more the merrier! Every child (and adult for that matter) that enters your household should be introduced to your Bulldog. If trustworthy neighbor children live nearby have them come in and spend time with your puppy if there is adult supervision. The children must understand that they may never over exert your puppy by playing too roughly or for too long a time.

Weather permitting, your puppy should go everywhere with you: the post office, the market, to the shopping mall—wherever. Be prepared to create a stir wherever you go because the very reason that attracted you to the first Bulldog you met applies to other people as well. Everyone will want to pet your little "Sourmug" and there is nothing in the world better for him.

The young Bulldog will quickly learn that all humans—young and old, short and tall, and of all races are friends. You are in charge. You must call the shots.

If your Bulldog has a show career in his future, there are other things in addition to just being handled that will have to be taught. All Bulldog show dogs must learn to have their mouth inspected by the judge. The judge must also be able to check the teeth. Males must be accustomed to having their testicles touched as the dog-show judge must determine that all male dogs are "complete." This means there are two normal sized testicles in the scrotum. These inspections must begin in puppyhood and be done on a regular and continuing basis.

THE ADOLESCENT BULLDOG

Bulldogs mature very slowly. While some breeds are mature at 12 months and most at 24 months, the Bulldog is fast approaching 36 months before most consider it finished with all those "stages." Some lines, however, may achieve maturity a bit earlier.

Bulldogs go through growth periods in "spurts." Parts of the anatomy seem to develop independently of each other so that a Bulldog puppy may look one way today and still another the following week. The little tank may take on the look of space rocket practically over night. Despair not. Eventually your puppy

Film and television star Ed Asner is a devoted Bulldog fan.

will undoubtedly revert back to what it gave promise of at six weeks.

Many breeds that have descended from the Mastiff (like the Bulldog) experience adolescent skin problems. Your veterinarian can recommend various products to assist you and your Bulldog through this period but the bottom line of course is keeping your Bulldog clean. Just remember that although the Bulldog is shorthaired, the coat requires constant care and attention.

Food needs change during this growth period. Think of Bulldog puppies as individualistic as children and act accordingly. The amount of food you give your Bulldog should be adjusted to how much it will consume at each meal and how that amount relates to optimum weight. Most Bulldogs are good eaters and you must be extremely careful not to let them get too fat. Some Bulldogs will

There is probably no better known Bulldog than the Kim Lindemoen-trained "Buford" who has starred in countless movies and television series. He is probably best known for his ongoing role in "Jake and the Fat Man" where he played the role of "Max."

It may seem as though a Bulldog's outlook on life is extremely serious, but they actually do have a wonderful sense of humor.

give you that forlorn look that says they are at starvation's doorstep regardless of how much food you give them. Excess weight for Bulldogs (or their owners for that matter!) can be lethal. If the entire meal is eaten quickly, add a small amount to the next feeding and continue to do so as the need increases. This method will insure you of giving your puppy enough food, but you must also pay close attention to your Bulldog's appearance.

At eight weeks of age, a Bulldog puppy is eating four meals a day. By the time he is six months old, the puppy can do well on two meals a day with perhaps a snack in the middle of the day. If your puppy does not eat the food offered, he is either not hungry or not well. Your dog will eat when he is hungry. If you suspect the dog is not well, a trip to the veterinarian is in order.

This adolescent period is a particularly important one, as it is the time your Bulldog must learn all the household and social rules by which he will live for the rest of his life. Your patience and commitment during this time will not only produce a respected canine good citizen but will forge a bond between the two of you that will grow and ripen into a wonderful relationship.

CARING for Your Bulldog

FEEDING AND NUTRITION

The best way to make sure your Bulldog puppy is obtaining the right amount and the correct type of food for his age is to follow the diet sheet provided by the breeder from whom you obtain your puppy. Do your best not to change the puppy's diet and you will be less apt to run into digestive problems and diarrhea. Diarrhea is very serious in young puppies. Puppies with diarrhea can dehydrate very rapidly causing severe problems and even death.

If it is necessary to change your Bulldog puppy's diet for any reason, it should be done gradually, over a period of several meals and a few days. Begin by adding a few tablespoons of the new food, gradually increasing the amount until the meal consists entirely of the new product.

By the time your Bulldog is 10 to 12 months old you can reduce feedings to one or at the most two a day. The main meal can be given either in the morning or evening. It is really a matter of choice on your part. There are two important things to remember: feed the main meal at the same time every day and make sure what you feed is nutritionally complete.

Bulldog puppies are notorious for getting themselves into trouble. Watch your puppy closely, especially when outdoors, so that nothing harms him.

Like father, like son. "Buford" introduces his son to the film colony.

Is there anything more British than the Bulldog? You would almost expect the family Bulldog to have a place setting in the proper British home.

The single meal can be supplemented by a morning or nighttime snack of hard dog biscuits made especially for medium-sized dogs. These biscuits not only become highly anticipated treats but are genuinely helpful in maintaining healthy gums and teeth.

"Balanced" Diets

In order for a canine diet to qualify as "complete and balanced" in the United States, it must meet standards set by the Subcommittee on Canine Nutrition of the National Research Council of the National Academy of Sciences. Most commercial foods manufactured for dogs meet these standards and prove this by listing the ingredients contained in the food on every package or can. The ingredients are listed in descending order with the main ingredient listed first.

Fed with any regularity at all, refined sugars can quickly cause your Bulldog to become obese and will definitely create tooth decay. Candy stores do not exist in nature and canine teeth are not genetically disposed to handling sugars. Do not feed your Bulldog candy or sweets and avoid products which contain sugar to any high degree.

Fresh water and a properly prepared, balanced diet containing the essential nutrients in correct proportions are all a healthy Bulldog needs to be offered. Dog foods come canned, dry, semi-moist, "scientifically fortified" and "all-natural." A visit to your local supermarket or pet store will reveal how vast an array you will be able to select from.

Always feed your Bulldog a high-quality food but not one that is high in protein. As far as protein content is concerned, your Bulldog should be on a diet recommended for seniors. While it is important to remember all dogs, whether toy or giant, are carnivorous (meat eating) animals, Bulldogs cannot tolerate foods that are extremely high in protein.

Beef, fed regularly, can create intestinal gas problems that are common to Bulldogs and a continual source of embarrassment to their owners. Lamb based food seems to agree with most Bulldogs. However, too much meat of any kind or a kibble too high in protein can also cause "hot spots." Hot spots are skin eruptions which cause severe itching that dogs will constantly scratch or chew until large open sores are created. If not attended to properly, the areas in which the skin has been broken begin to form moist, painful abscesses, all hair falls away and a veterinarian must be consulted.

Wild carnivores eat the entire beast they capture and kill. The carnivore's kills consist almost entirely of herbivores (plant eating) animals and invariably the carnivore begins its meal with the contents of the herbivore's stomach. This provides the carbohydrates, minerals and nutrients present in vegetables.

Four weeks old and beginning to eat nicely on their own. This is indeed a pleasant relief for Mama Bulldog who has given the pups her all.

Through centuries of domestication we have made our dogs entirely dependent upon us for their well being. Therefore we are entirely responsible for duplicating the food balance that wild dogs find in nature. The domesticated dog's diet must include some protein, carbohydrates, fats, roughage and small amounts of essential minerals and vitamins.

Finding commercially prepared diets which contain all the necessary nutrients in the proper balance will not present a problem. It is important to understand though, these commercially prepared foods do contain most of the nutrients your Bulldog requires. Most Bulldog breeders recommend vitamin supplementation for healthy coat and increased stamina, especially for show dogs, pregnant bitches or growing puppies.

Over-Supplementation

A great deal of controversy exists today regarding the orthopedic problems which afflict many breeds. Some claim these problems are entirely hereditary conditions but many others feel they can be exacerbated by overuse of mineral and vitamin supplements

The whole gang dives in at the milk bar. The authors' beloved "Emmy" and her amazing litter of ten living, breathing, and always hungry puppies.

"Whadda ya mean, it's your bowl?" Two Fairwood Bulldog pups have a serious discussion over property rights.

for puppies. Over-supplementation is now looked upon by some breeders as a major contributor to many skeletal abnormalities found in the purebred dogs of the day. In giving vitamin supplementation one should *never* exceed the prescribed amount. No vitamin, however, is a substitute for a nutritious balanced diet.

Pregnant and lactating bitches do require supplementation of some kind but here again it is not a case of "if a little is good, a lot would be a great deal better." Extreme caution is advised in this case and best discussed with your veterinarian.

If the owner of a Bulldog normally eats healthy nutritious food, there is no reason why his dog cannot be given some table scraps. What could possibly be harmful in good nutritious food?

Table scraps should be given only as part of the dog's meal and never from the table. A Bulldog that becomes accustomed to being hand fed from the table can become a real pest at meal time very quickly. Dinner guests may also find that the pleading stare and vocalization of your Bulldog is less than appealing when dinner is being served.

Dogs do not care if food looks like a hot dog or a piece of cheese. Truly nutritious dog foods are seldom manufactured to look like food that appeals to humans. Dogs only care about how food smells and tastes. It is highly doubtful you will be eating your dog's food so do not waste your money on these "looks just like" products.

Special Diets

There are now any number of commercially prepared diets for dogs with special dietary needs. The overweight, underweight or geriatric dog can have its nutritional needs met as can puppies and growing dogs. The calorie content of these foods is adjusted accordingly. With the correct amount of the right foods and the proper amount of exercise, your Bulldog should stay in top shape. Again, common sense must prevail. Too many calories will increase weight, too few will reduce weight.

Occasionally a young Bulldog going through the teething period will become a poor eater. The concerned owner's first response is to tempt the dog by handfeeding special treats and foods that the problem eater seems to prefer. This practice only serves to compound the problem. Once your dog learns to play the waiting game, he will turn up his nose at anything other than his favorite food knowing full well what he wants to eat will eventually arrive.

Unlike humans, dogs have no suicidal tendencies. A healthy dog will not starve itself to death. He may not eat enough to keep

There is absolutely nothing better for a Bulldog puppy than exposure to the sights and sounds of household living. They quickly learn to take even the most unusual events in stride.

Hot summer months demand special care for the Bulldog. Keeping your Bulldog cool and avoiding overexertion are paramount.

him in the shape we find ideal and attractive but he will definitely eat enough to maintain himself. If your Bulldog is not eating properly and appears to be too thin, it is probably best to consult your veterinarian.

SPECIAL NEEDS OF THE BULLDOG

Heat and Your Bulldog

Bulldogs are a man-made breed, as are all purebred dogs, but man has fashioned this breed in such a way that it requires very special care in hot weather. Anyone who wants a Bulldog must clearly understand these needs and be willing to accept responsibility for whatever measures must be taken to insure their completion.

Regular exercise and play are important parts of keeping your Bulldog puppy in good health.

Our hard and fast rule regarding Bulldogs and heat is no exertion or playing when temperatures are up and humidity is high. If a Bulldog begins to pant, steps must be taken immediately to cool it down. If panting is allowed to continue unchecked phlegm builds up in the Bulldog's throat and the tissues of the throat begin to swell. This causes stress and panting increases to the point where the throat swells shut and the dog dies of asphyxiation.

Should this condition begin to set in, the throat can be cleared by reaching down into the throat and pulling out the thick mucus that has accumulated. Experienced Bulldog owners keep phlegm-cutting liquids close at hand at all times. The small plastic containers of lemon juice sold at grocery stores, cola or lemon-lime soft drinks are all capable of cutting the phlegm loose and will allow the dog to vomit the loosened congested fluids.

If your Bulldog is in this distressed state, get him to a veterinarian at once. The first thing the veterinarian must do is give an injection to decrease the swelling in the throat and then cool the dog down. The most satisfactory solution to this problem is to be constantly aware of it and avoid allowing your Bulldog to become involved in any situation in which it can become distressed.

Travel

Heat problems encountered while traveling can be minimized with air-conditioned cars. However, for years we traveled with Bulldogs without the aid of air conditioning in any of our vehicles. We always took a cooler filled with ice and towels. Several days before we left we put water in plastic gallon milk jugs and froze it.

If the weather was warm we wrapped the jugs in towels and put the jugs right into the wire traveling crate the dog was in. The dogs did everything possible to lie right on the jugs. We also wet towels and put them over the crate and opened all windows

Your Bulldog puppy will be dependent on you for his good health for the rest of his life.

wide so that the air blew through the wet towel and cooled the dog.

Never stop in hot weather if you have to turn off the air conditioning in your car until you get where you are going. Once you arrive, get your Bulldog into air conditioned quarters without delay.

Never leave your dog in situation where he cannot get out of direct sunlight. Should you be forced to keep your Bulldog in the sun for a brief period, put a wet towel over the dog's body and head and keep him off asphalt or concrete.

If there is no air conditioning at your destination, gradually increase the temperature in your car so that you will not have to take your Bulldog from a cold vehicle into high heat. This is too much of a shock and the dog will start panting immediately. Needless to say, you must never leave your Bulldog alone in an automobile. Even on overcast days temperatures can soar in just minutes.

Small battery-operated fans can be obtained in many appliance shops that can be of great assistance in keeping your Bulldog cool. They are well worth the small investment and could be instrumental in avoiding serious complications.

While you might consider taking your Bulldog along on your summer vacation think the situation out carefully. It will take a great deal of prior planning and restrict your freedom considerably. Your Bulldog is much better off staying home where he can be carefully supervised. Should the need arise to leave your dog at a boarding kennel do not consider leaving him anywhere that has

Bulldogs are very sensitive to extreme heat and therefore this must be guarded against whenever outdoors.

not had documented experience in taking care of Bulldogs. Your breeder or veter-inarian may be able to make these recommend-ations.

If air travel is on your Bulldog's schedule discuss this with your veterinarian. He or she might advise tran-quilizing your dog to preclude stress. Oxygen deprivation during flights is a serious threat to your Bulldog. Further, most baggage attendants have no idea how dangerous it is to allow your Bulldog's shipping container to sit on the tarmac in the Summer sun.

Daily exercise will only benefit your older Bulldog. Why not join in on his routine?

No matter how many dogs you may have owned in the past, when it comes to Bulldogs and heat—the situation is entirely different!

Exercise

With everything said about Bulldogs and heat it may sound as if they should never be allowed outside of an air-conditioned room. This is not so. Proper exercise in the cool of the morning or evening is as vital to the Bulldog's longevity as is proper nutrition.

If your own exercise proclivities lie closer to a walk around the block than to ten-mile runs, your choice of a Bulldog was probably a wise one. The Bulldog is not a breed that requires taking your energy level to its outer limits. If your Bulldog shares its life with children or another dog it may well be getting all the exercise it needs to stay fit. Of course this should be supervised at all times.

Still, this does not mean that your Bulldog will not benefit from a daily walk around the park or around the block. On the contrary, moderated steady exercise that keeps your Bulldog's heart rate in the low working area will do nothing but extend his life. If your Bulldog is doing all this with you at his side, you are increasing the chances that the two of you will enjoy each other's company for many more years to come.

The bottom line of course is using your good judgment and your dog's reaction to moderate exercise. Naturally it should be done in the cool of morning or after sundown and then only when temperatures permit. Done at the proper time and building gradually, there is absolutely no reason why you and your Bulldog should not be able to work up to a daily mile walk at a reasonable rate of speed.

Toys and Chewing

Bulldogs, even as puppies have great jaw strength for their size and can be very destructive during their teething period. It is said that a Bulldog puppy is part private investigator and part vacuum cleaner. A puppy can find things that have yet to be lost and feel everything he finds should be filed in his tummy.

"Puppy-proofing" your home is a must. Your Bulldog will be ingenious in getting into things he shouldn't, so you have to be far more clever and keep ahead of what your puppy might get himself into.

Provide toys that will keep the puppy busy and eliminate his need for eating your needlepoint pillow or the legs off your favorite table. Just be sure to provide things that are hard to chew up such as the original Nylabone®, never anything gummy or soft. Rawhide, no matter what size and shape when new, eventually flattens out and can become lodged in the throat as can beef jerky or hot dogs.

Bulldog puppies love toys but never give a Bulldog anything to play with that he can fit into his mouth or break up into little pieces.

Your Bulldog should be accustomed to everyday events and all sorts of people—especially children.

Do not give your Bulldog meat bones unless they are the huge beef-knuckle bones and even they are risky. Bulldogs can chew up almost anything and may get a perforated or compacted intestine from it.

You will want to have a large bottle of liquid anti-chewing agent to put on things you do not want your Bulldog to chew on. These products can be purchased at local pet stores. Most dogs loathe the taste of these, but they prove to be harmless to the dog.

Bulldogs love shoes of all types and will often grab at the shoes you are wearing as you are walking along. This is hazardous to both your dog and you. Never give your puppy old shoes to play with. A dog can see no difference between an old sneaker you have given him and a brand new one. Once you've worn shoes, they smell exactly alike to your Bulldog—age and cost not withstanding!

Socialization

The Bulldog is by nature a happy dog and takes most situations in stride, but it is important to accommodate the breed's natural instincts by making sure your dog is accustomed to everyday events of all kinds. Traffic, strange noises, loud or hyperactive children and strange animals can be very intimidating to a dog of any breed that has never experienced them before. Gently and gradually introduce your puppy to as many strange situations as you possibly can.

Make it a practice to take your Bulldog with you everywhere whenever practical. The breed is a real crowd pleaser and you will find your dog will savor all the attention it gets.

ILLNESS AND INJURY

One problem we have with Bulldogs is that their threshold of pain is extremely high. This seems as if it would be a real plus but it most definitely is not. Because it takes a Bulldog so long to show visible signs of pain and discomfort, by the time you realize it is ill or may have sustained an internal injury, the dog could be in the critical stage. For this reason we strongly recommend you have a veterinarian that understands this situation. If the veterinarian tries conservative treatment on your Bulldog, it may be fatal.

Veterinarians who are not experienced with Bulldogs may think that because the dog may just have started exhibiting symptoms, the problem has just started. This is not true. The problem could easily have started some time before, perhaps even days before, but your Bulldog is just at the point of letting you know about it. You must act immediately if your Bulldog appears to be ill and your vet must use aggressive methods of treatment.

BATHING AND GROOMING

Although the Bulldog does not have a long coat to contend with, the breed is no less in need of grooming. This is a breed that needs to be taken care of. It is like having a child in the family.

Bulldogs are unable to wash their own tails, so their owners must attend to this. Nor can Bulldogs take care of their wrinkles which can become irritated very easily if not cleaned on at least a weekly basis. Unscented "baby wipes" are excellent for this job. The tail and the area beneath it must be washed and dried. This must be done with the Bulldog's wrinkles as well. Only use tearless dog shampoo. Do not use human baby shampoo as it is too harsh. If there is any irritation this needs to be treated with an ointment that can be obtained from your veterinarian.

All Bulldogs shed 365 days a year and if for no other reason, daily brushings will help avoid problems the breed is susceptible to. Brushing assists this process.

Nail Trimming

Bulldogs seldom get enough exercise on rough surfaces to wear their nails down and these have to be clipped or filed down on a regular basis.

This is also a good time to accustom your dog to having its feet inspected. Always inspect your dog's feet for cracked pads. Pay particular attention to any swollen or tender areas. Check between the toes for splinters and thorns and the Bulldog nemesis—interdigital cysts. These cysts are common in Bulldogs and should be called to the attention of your veterinarian as soon as they are detected.

The nails of a Bulldog can grow long very quickly. Do not allow the nails to become overgrown and then expect to cut them back easily. Each nail has a blood vessel running through the center called the "quick." The quick grows close to the end of the nail and contains very sensitive nerve endings. If the nail is allowed to grow too long it will be impossible to cut it back to a proper length without cutting into the quick. This causes

Do not encourage your Bulldog to develop bad habits like going after shoes (both on and off feet).

severe pain to the dog and can also result in a great deal of bleeding that can be very difficult to stop.

Nails can be trimmed with canine nail clippers, an electric nail grinder or coarse file made expressly for that purpose. All three of these items can be purchased at major pet emporiums.

We prefer the electric nail grinder above the others because it is so easy to control and helps avoid cutting into the quick. Dark nails make it practically impossible to see where the quick ends. Regardless of which nail trimming device is used, one must proceed with caution and remove only a small portion of the nail at a time.

Use of the electric grinder requires introducing your puppy to it at an early age. The instrument has a whining sound to it not unlike a dentist's drill. The noise combined with the vibration of the sanding head on the nail itself can take some getting used to, but most dogs we have used it on eventually accept it as one of life's trials. Most Bulldogs do not like having their nails trimmed no matter what device is used. Our own eventual decision is to use the grinder as it is less apt to damage the quick.

Should the quick be nipped in the trimming process, there are any number of blood clotting products available at pet shops that will almost immediately stem the flow of blood. It is wise to have one of these products on hand in case there is a nail trimming accident or the dog tears a nail on its own.

If brushing is attended to regularly, bathing will seldom be necessary unless your Bulldog finds its way into something that leaves its coat with a disagreeable odor. Even then, there are many products, both dry and liquid, available at your local pet store that eliminate odors and leave the coat shiny and clean.

A damp washcloth will put the Bulldog that has

A good belly rub will make you and your Bulldog best friends for life!

Check your Bulldog's ears regularly for dirt, debris, and any foul odor. Keep your dog's ears free from debris at all times to avoid infection.

given itself a mud bath back in shape very quickly. However, should your Bulldog's coat become wet in cold weather, be sure to towel down the dog thoroughly. The Bulldog is a thin-coated breed and has no undercoat to protect it from a draft or winter chill.

Brushing should always be done in the same direction as the hair grows. You should begin at the dog's head brushing toward the tail and down the sides and legs. This procedure will loosen the dead hair and brush it off the dog.

Check the skin inside the thighs and armpits to see if it is dry or red. Artificial heat during winter months can dry out the skin and cause it to become chapped. Place a small amount of petroleum jelly or baby oil on the palms of your hands and rub your hands over the dry areas.

Bulldogs are subject to dry noses. In extreme cases the nose leather can shrivel and crack. Avoid this by regular applications of petroleum jelly.

HOUSETRAINING and Training

There is no breed of dog that cannot be trained. Some breeds appear to be more difficult to get the desired response from than others. Bulldogs are certainly a case in point. However, this is more apt to be due to the trainer not being "Bulldog specific" in his or her approach to the training, than the dog's inability to learn.

Ease of training depends in a great part upon just how much a dog depends upon his master's approval. The entirely dependent dog lives to please his master and will do everything in his power to evoke the approval response from the person he is devoted to.

At the opposite end of the pole we have a totally independent dog who is not remotely concerned with what his master thinks. Dependency varies from one breed to the next and within breeds as well. Bulldogs are no exception to this rule. While Bulldogs are entirely dependent upon their owners for all their physical needs they are extremely intelligent and they fiercely maintain their psychological independence.

Successfully training a Bulldog depends upon your fully understanding the breed's character and dealing with it accordingly.

Some professionals who train dogs advise obtaining a puppy on the 49th day of his life. Their research indicates it is at this precise point in time that a puppy is most ready to bond to a human and subsequently depend upon that person for approval. Prior to that time the puppy needs to be with its siblings and mother. Just after the 49th day the puppy passes through varying stages which make it less ideal for human bonding and more independent in nature.

Take your puppy to the same place to eliminate every time you go outside.

We are sure not all behaviorists will

To keep new puppies happy while in their exercise pen or crate, give them plenty of toys to chew on.

ascribe to the 49th day theory, but there does seem to be general agreement that the optimum time to bring a puppy into his new home is at about seven to eight weeks of age. It is wise to at least consider this information and discuss it with the breeder from whom you will be purchasing your puppy.

The key to having a well-trained Bulldog is to start as a very young puppy with play training. While it may be difficult to remind ourselves that our wonderful "Sourmugs" trace back to the wolf, doing so will help in understanding our dogs. The wolf mother plays with her cubs and part of that play results in teaching the cubs what they may and may not do. The Bulldog puppy, like its wolf cub ancestor, must think it is having fun and has decided on its own to do what it is participating in. The minute you try to force Bulldogs to do something, or to stop doing something they are accustomed to doing, they begin to assert their independence and you may set up what could be a lifelong battle of wills. Never allow a Bulldog puppy to do something that you would not want a 50 to 60 pound adult to do.

When playing with your Bulldog puppy, always practice good manners and never allow bad habits to form.

While a puppy biting your hands or feet, refusing to give up a toy or jumping on you—rough play of any kind—may appear cute and funny, you are actually encouraging the behavior and making it harder to train him not to.

The problem with battles of will is that the Bulldog's history of tenacity is then called forth and the dog becomes an immovable object. When this immovable object (the Bulldog) meets the irresistible force (its owner) well, little more need be said!

You should never strike a Bulldog. For one thing, it does no good, and another, it may make the dog aggressive. You do not ever want to encourage aggressiveness in a Bulldog.

This is not to say there are to be no rules or regulations in Bulldog training. On the contrary, it is very important to train a Bulldog to be absolutely confident of its place in the "pack." The Bulldog's place in the pecking order must be below every family member and this must be clear to the dog from the first day he enters his new home.

Housetraining

Without a doubt the best way to housetrain a Bulldog is to use the "crate method." First-time dog owners are inclined to initially see the crate or cage method of housetraining as cruel but those same people will return later and thank me profusely for having suggested it in the first place. All dogs need a place of their own to retreat to and you will find the Bulldog will consider its cage that place.

Use of a crate reduces house-training time down to an absolute minimum and avoids keeping a puppy under constant stress by incessantly correcting it for making mistakes in the house. The anti-crate advocates consider it cruel to confine a puppy for any length of time but find no problem in constantly harassing and punishing the puppy because it has wet on the carpet and relieved itself behind the sofa.

The crate used for housetraining should only be large enough for the puppy to stand up and lie down in and stretch out comfortably. These crates are available at most pet shops at a wide range of prices. It is not necessary to dash out and buy a new crate every few weeks to accommodate the Bulldog's rapid spurts of growth. Simply cut a piece of plywood of a size to partition off the excess space in the very large cage and move it back as needed.

Begin using the crate to feed your puppy in. Keep the door closed and latched while the puppy is eating. When the meal is

A Bulldog will not soil his bed or living quarters. He will also try to signal his owners at every possible opportunity when he has to go out.

finished, open the cage and carry the puppy outdoors to the spot where you want him to learn to eliminate. As you are doing so you should consistently use the same words. Whether the words are "go out," "potty" or what ever, makes no difference. The important point is the puppy will be learning both where to eliminate and that certain words mean something is expected.

In the event you do not have outdoor access or will be away from home for long periods of time, begin housetraining by placing newspapers in some out of the way corner that is easily accessible for the puppy. If you consistently take your puppy to the same spot, you will reinforce the habit of going there for that purpose.

It is important that you do not let the puppy loose after eating. Young puppies will eliminate almost immediately after eating or drinking. They will also be ready to relieve themselves when they first wake up and after playing. If you keep a watchful eye on your puppy you will quickly learn when this is about to take place. A puppy usually circles and sniffs the floor just before it will relieve itself. Do not give your puppy an opportunity to learn that it can eliminate in the house! Your house training chores will be reduced considerably if you avoid bad habits beginning in the first place.

If you are not able to watch your puppy every minute, it should be in its crate with the door securely latched. Each time you put your puppy in the crate give it a small treat of some kind. Throw

Once your Bulldog is housetrained, there will be no mistaking his "I want to go out" look.

If you are unable to watch your puppy every minute, he should be in his cage or another safe location where he cannot get into mischief.

the treat to the back of the crate and encourage the puppy to walk in on its own. When it does so, praise the puppy and perhaps hand it another piece of the treat through the wires of the cage.

Do not succumb to your puppy's complaints about being in its crate. The puppy must learn to stay in its crate and to do so without unnecessary complaining. A quick "no" command and a tap on the crate will usually get the puppy to understand theatrics will not result in liberation.

Do understand a puppy of eight to twelve weeks will not be able to contain itself for long periods of time. Puppies of that age must relieve themselves every few hours except at night. Your schedule must be adjusted accordingly. Also make sure your puppy has relieved itself both bowel and bladder the last thing at night and do not dawdle when you wake up in the morning.

Your first priority in the morning is to get the puppy outdoors. Just how early this ritual will take place will depend much more upon your puppy than upon you. If your Bulldog is like most others there will be no doubt in your mind when it needs to be let out. You will also very quickly learn to tell the difference between the "this is an emergency" complaint and the "I just want out" grumbling. Do not test the young puppy's ability to contain itself. Its vocal demand to be let out is confirmation that the housetraining lesson is being learned.

If you find it necessary to be away from home all day, you will not be able to leave your puppy in a crate, but on the other hand, do not make the mistake of allowing it to roam the house or even a large room at will. Confine the puppy to a small room or partitioned-off area and cover the floor with newspaper. Make this area large enough so that the puppy will not have to relieve itself next to its bed, food or water bowls. You will soon find the puppy will be inclined to use one particular spot to perform its bowel and bladder functions. When you are home you must take the puppy to this exact spot to eliminate at the appropriate time.

BASIC TRAINING

Early "puppy kindergarten" along with puppy play training are vital if you plan to do obedience work of any kind. Most Bulldogs could probably get their Companion Dog (CD) titles if their owner had patience. A Bulldog's trainer has to understand how a Bulldog sees life. Most Bulldogs would assume that if their owner is capable of throwing an object, he or she would be just as capable of bringing it back. Retrieving is not something a Bulldog would think to do on its own. Nor would most Bulldogs see a good reason to jump a bar or solid jump when they can simply walk through or around it more easily. The human trainer has to be absolutely dedicated, have a good sense of humor and the patience of Jobe.

There are a few Bulldogs who have their Utility Dog (UD) and Tracking Dog Excellent (TDX) titles—but very few! My hat is off to their trainers.

It is said that exceptions prove the rule and if this is so Kim Lindemoen, whose business is training dogs and animals of all kinds, has had amazing success with training Bulldogs. Her "Bufford" is not only an AKC champion with a Canine Good Citizen title, he is an international star of both television and

Walking on lead is one of the most important lessons your Bulldog will ever learn. Accustom your puppy to a leash while he is young so that you will have no problems when he is an adult.

movies! Bufford is probably best known to his many fans as "Max" on the TV series "Jake and the Fat Man" but he has had important roles in many other films and television shows as well. Where you are emotionally and the environment in which you train are just as important to your dog's training as is its state of mind at the time. Never begin training when you are irritated, distressed or preoccupied. Nor should you begin basic training in a place which interferes with you or your dog's concentration. Once the commands are understood and learned you can begin testing your dog in public places but at first the two of you should work in a place where you can concentrate fully upon each other.

The "No!" Command

There is no doubt whatsoever that one of the most important commands your Bulldog puppy will ever learn is the meaning of the "no!" command. It is critical that the puppy learn this command just as soon as possible. One important piece of advice in using this and all other commands—never give a command you are not prepared and able to follow through on! The only way a puppy learns to obey commands is to realize that once issued, commands must be complied with. Learning the "no" command should start on the first day of the puppy's arrival at your home.

Puppies have a very short attention span, so make each training session short and always end on a positive note.

Leash Training

It is never too early to accustom the Bulldog puppy to a collar and leash. It is your way of keeping your dog under control. It may not be necessary for the puppy or adult Bulldog to wear its collar and identification tags within the confines of your home but no Bulldog should ever leave home without a collar and without the leash held securely in your hand.

Begin getting your Bulldog puppy accustomed to its collar by leaving it on for a few minutes at a time. Gradually extend the time you leave the collar on. Most Bulldogs become accustomed to their collar very quickly and forget they are even wearing one.

Once this is accomplished, attach a lightweight leash to the collar while you are playing with the puppy. Do not try to guide the puppy at first. The point here is to accustom the puppy to the feeling of having something attached to the collar.

Some Bulldog puppies adapt to their collar very quickly and without any undo resistance learn to be guided with the leash. Other Bulldog puppies may be absolutely adamant that they will not have any part of leash training and seem intent on strangling themselves before submitting.

Should your puppy be one of the latter do not continue to force the issue. Simply create a "lasso" with your leash and put your Bulldog's head and front legs through the lasso opening so that the leash encircles the puppy's shoulders and chest, just behind the front legs. Young Bulldogs seem to object less to this method than having the leash around their neck.

Encourage your puppy to follow you as you move away. Should the puppy be reluctant to cooperate, coax it along with a treat of some kind. Hold the treat in front of the puppy's nose to encourage him to follow you. Just as soon as the puppy takes a few steps toward you praise him enthusiastically and continue to do so as you continue to move along.

Make the initial sessions very brief and very enjoyable. Continue the lessons in your home or yard until the puppy is completely unconcerned about the fact that he is on a leash. With a treat in one hand and the leash in the other you can begin to use both to guide the puppy in the direction you wish to go.

Once the leash around the body is taken in stride and the puppy has become accustomed to walking along with you, you can start attaching the leash to your puppy's collar. Your walks can begin in front of the house and eventually extend down the street and around the block. This is one lesson no puppy is too young to learn.

The "Come" Command

The next most important lesson for the Bulldog puppy to learn is to come when called, therefore is very important that the puppy learn his name as soon as possible. Constant repetition is what does the trick in teaching a puppy his name. Use the name every time you talk to your puppy.

Learning to "come" on command could save your Bulldog's life when the two of you venture out into the world. "Come" is the command a dog must understand has to be obeyed without question but the dog should not associate that command with fear. Your dog's response to its name and the word "come" should always be associated with a pleasant experience such as great praise and petting or particularly in the case of the Bulldog—a food treat.

In Bulldog training it is far easier to avoid the establishment of bad habits than it is to correct them once set. Never give the "come" command unless you are sure your Bulldog puppy will come to you. The very young puppy is far more inclined to respond to learning the "come" command than the older Bulldog. Use the command initially when the puppy is already on his way to you or give the command while walking or running away from the youngster. Clap your hands and sound very happy and excited about having the puppy join in on this "game."

The very young Bulldog will normally want to stay as close to his owner as possible, especially in strange surroundings. When your puppy sees you moving away, his natural inclination will be to get close to you. This is a perfect time to use the "come" command.

Later, as the puppy grows more independent and more headstrong as you now know a Bulldog can do, you may want to attach a long leash or rope to the puppy's collar to ensure the correct response. Do not chase or punish your puppy for not obeying the "come" command. Doing so in the initial stages of training makes the youngster associate the command with something to resist and this will result in avoidance rather than the immediate positive response you desire. It is imperative that you praise your Bulldog puppy and give him a treat when he does come to you, even if it voluntarily delays responding for many minutes.

The "Sit" and "Stay" Commands

Just as important to your Bulldog's safety (and your sanity!) as the "no!" command and learning to come when called are the "sit" and "stay" commands. Even very young Bulldogs can learn the sit command quickly, especially if it appears to be a game and a food treat is involved.

First, remember the Bulldog-in-training should always be on collar and leash for all his lessons. A Bulldog is certainly not beyond getting up and walking away when he has decided enough is too much!

In training most dogs the trainer would give the "sit" command immediately before pushing down on your Bulldog hindquarters. Pushing down on the rear quarters does not work real well with Bulldogs. They have a strong tendency to resist any force.

A much better way is to take your left hand or forearm (depending upon the size of the dog) and place it across the back

Kim and Burt Lindemoen with a few famous "Kim's Exotic Critters" stars.

legs at the hocks. Then place your hand on the dog's chest. Holding the back legs where they are, push the dog back by applying pressure to the chest until the dog sits. Praise the dog lavishly when it does sit, even though it is you who made the action take place. Again, a food treat always seems to get the lesson across to the learning Bulldog.

Put your hand lightly on the dog's rear and repeat the "sit" command several times. If your dog makes an attempt to get up, repeat the command yet again while exerting pressure on the chest. Make your Bulldog stay in this position for increasing lengths of time. Begin with a few seconds and increase the time as lessons progress over the following weeks.

Should your Bulldog student attempt to get up or to lie down it should be corrected by simply saying, "sit!" in a firm voice. This should be accompanied by returning the dog to the desired position.

Once your Bulldog has begun to understand the "sit" command, you may be able to assume the position by simply putting your

Don't expect a very young Bulldog puppy to remember all of his lessons all of the time. Here Mick and Pam Mattson's "Sophie" looks as if she's trying to recall just what "no!" really means.

hand on the dog's chest and exerting slight backward pressure.

All of this should be done as gently as possible. It can really be next to impossible to push a Bulldog's rear end down without exerting so much pressure you could conceivably

The sit and stay commands are very important for your pet Bulldog to learn.

cause an injury to the dog's hips or stifle joints.

Only when you decide your dog should get up should it be allowed to do so. Do not test the young Bulldog's patience to the limits. Remember you are dealing with a baby and the attention span of any youngster is relatively short.

When you do decide the dog can get up, call his name, say "OK" and make a big fuss over it. Praise and a food treat are in order every time your Bulldog responds correctly.

Once your Bulldog has mastered the "sit" lesson you may start on the "stay" command. With your Bulldog on leash and facing you, command him to "sit," then take a step or two back. If your dog attempts to get up to follow firmly say, "Sit, stay!" While you are saying this raise your hand, palm toward the dog, and again command "Stay!"

Any attempt on your dog's part to get up must be corrected at once, returning him to the sit position and repeating, "Stay!" Once your dog begins to understand what you want, you can gradually increase the distance you step back. With a long leash attached to your dog's collar (even a clothesline will do) start with a few steps and gradually increase the distance to several yards. Your Bulldog must eventually learn the "Sit, stay" command must be obeyed no matter how far away you are. Later on, with advanced training, your dog will learn the command is to be obeyed even when you move entirely out of sight.

Avoid calling the dog to you at first. This makes the dog overly anxious to get up and run to you. Until your Bulldog masters the "sit" lesson and is able to remain in the sit position for as long as you dictate, walk back to your dog and say "OK" which is a signal that the command is over. Later, when your dog becomes more reliable in this respect, you can call him to you.

The "sit, stay" lesson can take considerable time and patience especially with the Bulldog puppy whose attention span will be very short. It is best to keep the "stay" part of the lesson to a minimum until the Bulldog is at least five or six-months old. Everything in a very young Bulldog's makeup will urge it to follow you wherever you go. Forcing a very young Bulldog to operate against his natural instincts can be bewildering for the puppy.

The "Down" Command

Once your Bulldog has mastered the "sit" and "stay" commands, you may begin work on "down." This is the single word command for lie down. Use the "down" command *only* when you want the dog to lie down. If you want your Bulldog to get off your sofa or to stop jumping up on people use the "off" command. Do not interchange these two commands. Doing so will only serve to confuse your dog and evoking the right response will become next to impossible.

The "down" position is especially useful if you want your Bulldog to remain in a particular place for a long period of time. A Bulldog is far more inclined to stay put when it is lying down than when he is sitting.

Teaching this command to your Bulldog may take more time and patience than the previous lessons the two of you have undertaken. It is believed by some animal behaviorists that assuming the "down" position somehow represents submissiveness to the dog. Considering the self-willed nature of our Bulldogs, it is easy to understand how this command could prove more difficult for them to comply with. In the end, once the "down" command has become a part of the Bulldog's repertory, it seems to be more relaxing for the dog and you will find it seems less inclined to get up and wander off.

With your Bulldog sitting in front of and facing you, hold a treat in your right hand with the excess part of the leash in your left hand. Hold the treat under the dog's nose and slowly bring your hand down to the ground. Your dog will follow the treat with his head and neck. As he does, give the command "down."

An alternative method of getting your Bulldog headed into the down position is to move around to the dog's right side and as you draw his attention downward with your right hand, slide your left arm under the dog's front legs and gently slide them forward. In the case of a small puppy you will undoubtedly have to be on your knees next to the youngster.

As your Bulldog's forelegs begin to slide out to its front, keep moving the treat along the ground until the dog's whole body is lying on the ground while you continually repeat "down." Once your dog has assumed the position you desire, give him the treat and a lot of praise. Continue assisting your Bulldog into the "down" position until he does so on his own. Be firm and be patient.

The "Heel" Command

In learning to heel, your Bulldog will walk on your left side with his shoulder next to your leg no matter which direction you might go or how quickly you turn. Teaching your Bulldog to heel will not only make your daily walks far more enjoyable, it will make a far more tractable companion when the two of you are in crowded or confusing situations. Bulldogs usually want to be with you wherever you go so training him to walk along in the correct position is usually not much of a problem.

We have found a link-chain training collar is very useful for the heeling lesson. It provides both quick pressure around the neck and a snapping sound, both of which get the dog's

Bulldogs rarely have trouble learning to lie down...one of the breed's most famous positions.

91

attention. Erroneously referred to as a "choke collar," the link-chain collar used properly will not choke the dog. The pet shop at which you purchase the training collar will be able to show you the proper way to put this collar on your dog.

As you train your Bulldog puppy to walk along on the leash, you should accustom the youngster to walk on your left side. The leash should cross your body from the dog's collar to your right hand. The excess portion of the leash will be folded into your right hand and your left hand on the leash will be used to make corrections with the leash.

A quick short jerk on the leash with your left hand will keep your Bulldog from lunging side to side, pulling ahead or lagging back. As you make a correction give the "heel" command. Always keep the leash slack as long as your dog maintains the proper position at your side.

If your dog begins to drift away give the leash a sharp jerk and guide the dog back to the correct position and give the "heel" command. *Do not pull on the lead with steady pressure!* You must be very careful of a Bulldog's throat. What is needed is a sharp but gentle jerking motion to get your Bulldog's attention. Remember, it is always "jerk and release."

Quick, short jerks with a training collar will correct your Bulldog when a misdeed is done.

A good Bulldog will never rest until he finds a solution to his problem.

Training Classes

There are actually few limits to what a patient, consistent Bulldog owner (and the accent is most definitely on patient and consistent!) can teach his or her dog. While the Bulldog may not leap to perform the first time you attempt to teach him something new, take heart. Once the lesson is mastered your Bulldog will perform with enthusiasm and gusto especially if he has learned all these "silly" things you have taught him to do are in reality fun and will result in a lot of fun and praise.

Don't forget, you are dealing with what could be one of the most stubborn breeds known to man. But also be aware that the Bulldog is one of the most intelligent and wonderful breeds of dog known to man. Your Bulldog performs because he has decided he wants to, not because you are forcing him to obey. Do not tell your Bulldog this, but if you are persistent enough in your training your Bulldog will eventually think the whole thing was his own idea in the first place!

For advanced obedience work beyond the basics it is wise for the Bulldog owner to consider local professional assistance. Professional trainers have had long standing experience in avoiding the pitfalls of obedience training and can help you to avoid them as well.

This training assistance can be obtained in many ways. The strange dogs and new people encountered at training classes are particularly good for your Bulldog's socialization. There are free-

Once your Bulldog has learned his basic manners, there are countless ways the two of you can enjoy daily activities.

of-charge classes at many parks and Recreation facilities, as well as very formal and sometimes very expensive individual lessons with private trainers.

There are also some obedience schools that will take your Bulldog and train him for you. However, unless your schedule provides no time at all to train your own dog, having someone else train the dog for you would be last on our list of recommendations. The rapport that develops between the owner who has trained his or her Bulldog to be a pleasant companion and good canine citizen is very special—well worth the time and patience it requires to achieve.

While you may not even be able to feel puppy bites, those little jaws soon develop a vice-like grip and the puppy teeth are replaced by those that can do incredible damage. Do not allow your puppy to chew on you or your clothing at any time.

VERSATILITY

Once your Bulldog has been taught his basic manners, there are countless ways that the two of you can participate in enjoyable events. The breed is highly successful in conformation shows and has proven it can also do well in obedience competition.

There are Canine Good Citizen certificates that can be earned through the American Kennel Club and Bulldogs have proven to be wonderful Therapy Dogs by visiting homes for the aged, orphanages and hospitals. Bulldogs love people and people are always interested in the breed because of its looks. It is amazing to see how kind and gentle some otherwise comical and rowdy Bulldogs will behave with people who are ill or feeble or with small children. It has been proven these visits provide great therapeutic value to patients.

The well-trained Bulldog can provide a whole world of activities for the owner. You are only limited by the amount of time you wish to invest in this remarkable breed.

SPORT of Purebred Dogs

Welcome to the exciting and sometimes frustrating sport of dogs. No doubt you are trying to learn more about dogs or you wouldn't be deep into this book. This section covers the basics that may entice you, further your knowledge and help you to understand the dog world.

Dog showing has been a very popular sport for a long time and has been taken quite seriously by some. Others only enjoy it as a hobby.

The Kennel Club in England was formed in 1859, the American Kennel Club was established in 1884 and the Canadian Kennel Club was formed in 1888. The purpose of these clubs was to register purebred dogs and maintain their Stud Books. In the beginning, the concept of registering dogs was not readily accepted. More than 36 million dogs have been enrolled in the AKC Stud Book since its inception in 1888. Presently the kennel clubs not only register dogs but adopt and enforce rules and regulations governing dog shows, obedience trials and field trials. Over the years they have fostered and encouraged interest in the health and welfare of the purebred dog. They routinely donate funds to veterinary research for study on genetic disorders.

Below are the addresses of the kennel clubs in the United States, Great Britain and Canada.

The American Kennel Club
260 Madison Avenue
New York, NY 10016
or 5580 Centerview Drive,
Raleigh, NC 27606

The Kennel Club
1 Clarges Street
Picadilly, London, W1Y 8AB, England

The Canadian Kennel Club
89 Skyway Avenue
Suite 100
Etobicoke, Ontario, Canada M9W 6R4

Today there are numerous activities that are enjoyable for both the dog and the handler. Some of the activities include conformation showing, obedience competition, tracking, agility, the Canine Good Citizen Certificate, and a wide range of instinct tests that vary from breed to breed. Where you start depends upon your goals which early on may not be readily apparent.

PUPPY KINDERGARTEN

Every puppy will benefit from this class. PKT is the foundation for all future dog activities from conformation to "couch potatoes." Pet owners should make an effort to attend even if they never expect to show their dog. The class is designed for puppies about three months of age with graduation at approximately five months of age. All the puppies will be in the same age group and, even though some may be a little unruly, there should not be any real problem. This class will teach the puppy some beginning obedience. As in all obedience classes the owner learns how to train his own dog. The PKT class gives the puppy the opportunity to interact with other puppies in the same age group and exposes him to strangers, which is very important. Some dogs grow up with behavior problems, one of them being fear of strangers. As you can see, there can be much to gain from this class.

All puppies who participate in puppy kindergarten training will benefit. Aside from the training they receive, it is a great way for them to socialize with other dogs.

There are some basic obedience exercises that every dog should learn. Some of these can be started with puppy kindergarten.

CONFORMATION

Conformation showing is our oldest dog show sport. This type of showing is based on the dog's appearance—that is his structure, movement and attitude. When considering this type of showing, you need to be aware of your breed's standard and be able to evaluate your dog compared to that standard. The breeder of your puppy or other experienced breeders would be good sources for such an evaluation. Puppies can go through lots of changes over a period of time. Many puppies start out as promising hopefuls and then after maturing may be disappointing as show candidates. Even so this should not deter them from being excellent pets.

Usually conformation training classes are offered by the local kennel or obedience clubs. These are excellent places for training puppies. The puppy should be able to walk on a lead before entering such a class. Proper ring procedure and technique for posing (stacking) the dog will be demonstrated as well as gaiting the dog. Usually certain patterns are used in the ring such as the triangle or the "L." Conformation class, like the PKT class, will give your youngster the opportunity to socialize with different breeds of dogs and humans too.

It takes some time to learn the routine of conformation showing. Usually one starts at the puppy matches that may be AKC Sanctioned or Fun Matches. These matches are generally for puppies from two or three months to a year old, and there may be

Puppies that are two to three months of age to one year old may participate in AKC-sanctioned puppy matches.

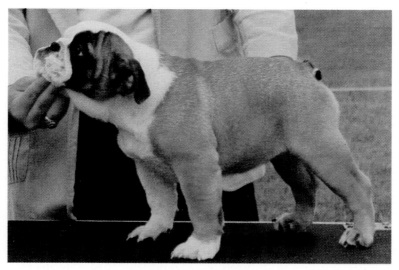

Ho-Jo's Come From Behind, adorable puppy bred and owned by Dr. John and Hope Jones of San Jose, California, pictured winning Best in Match with Dr. Jones handling.

classes for the adult over the age of 12 months. Similar to point shows, the classes are divided by sex and after completion of the classes in that breed or variety, the class winners compete for Best of Breed or Variety. The winner goes on to compete in the Group and the Group winners compete for Best in Match. No championship points are awarded for match wins.

A few matches can be great training for puppies even though there is no intention to go on showing. Matches enable the puppy to meet new people and be handled by a stranger—the judge. It is also a change of environment, which broadens the horizon for both dog and handler. Matches and other dog activities boost the confidence of the handler and especially the younger handlers.

Earning an AKC championship is built on a point system, which is different from Great Britain. To become an AKC Champion of Record the dog must earn 15 points. The number of points earned each time depends upon the number of dogs in competition. The number of points available at each show depends upon the breed, its sex and the location of the show. The United States is divided into ten AKC zones. Each zone has its own set of points. The purpose of the zones is to try to equalize the points available from breed to breed and area to area. The AKC adjusts the point scale annually.

The number of points that can be won at a show are between one and five. Three-, four- and five-point wins are considered majors. Not only does the dog need 15 points won under three different judges, but those points must include two majors under two different judges. Canada also works on a point system but majors are not required.

Dogs always show before bitches. The classes available to those seeking points are: Puppy (which may be divided into 6 to 9 months and 9 to 12 months); 12 to 18 months; Novice; Bred-by-Exhibitor; American-bred; and Open. The class winners of the same sex of each breed or variety compete against each other for Winners Dog and Winners Bitch. A Reserve Winners Dog and Reserve Winners Bitch are also awarded but do not carry any points unless the Winners win is disallowed by AKC. The Winners Dog and Bitch compete with the specials (those dogs that have attained championship) for Best of Breed or Variety, Best of Winners and Best of Opposite Sex. It is possible to pick up an extra point or even a major if the points are higher for the defeated winner than those of Best of Winners. The latter would get the higher total from the defeated winner.

At an all-breed show, each Best of Breed or Variety winner will go on to his respective Group and then the Group winners will compete against each other for Best in Show. There are seven Groups: Sporting, Hounds, Working, Terriers, Toys, Non-Sporting

Smasher Sinclair wins Best of Opposite Sex at the Chicago Bulldog Club Puppy Match at just four months of age. Handled by Gail Warta for this win under judge Richard Markley.

and Herding. Obviously there are no Groups at speciality shows (those shows that have only one breed or a show such as the American Spaniel Club's Flushing Spaniel Show, which is for all flushing spaniel breeds).

Earning a championship in England is somewhat different since they do not have a point system. Challenge Certificates are awarded if the judge feels the dog is de-

Ch. Bullseyes Hustler owned by Joan Harding of Howell, New Jersey. This picture shows Hustler winning under Bulldog breeder Robert Hetherington when just 7 1/2 months old.

serving regardless of the number of dogs in competition. A dog must earn three Challenge Certificates under three different judges, with at least one of these Certificates being won after the age of 12 months. Competition is very strong and entries may be higher than they are in the U.S. The Kennel Club's Challenge Certificates are only available at Championship Shows.

In England, The Kennel Club regulations require that certain dogs, Border Collies and Gundog breeds, qualify in a working capacity (i.e., obedience or field trials) before becoming a full Champion. If they do not qualify in the working aspect, then they are designated a Show Champion, which is equivalent to the AKC's Champion of Record. A Gundog may be granted the title of Field Trial Champion (FT Ch.) if it passes all the tests in the field but would also have to qualify in conformation before becoming a full Champion. A Border Collie that earns the title of Obedience Champion (Ob Ch.) must also qualify in the conformation ring before becoming a Champion.

The U.S. doesn't have a designation full Champion but does award for Dual and Triple Champions. The Dual Champion must be a Champion of Record, and either Champion Tracker, Herding Champion, Obedience Trial Champion or Field Champion. Any dog that has been awarded the titles of Champion of Record, and any two of the following: Champion

Tracker, Herding Champion, Obedience Trial Champion or Field Champion, may be designated as a Triple Champion.

The shows in England seem to put more emphasis on breeder judges than those in the U.S. There is much competition within the breeds. Therefore the quality of the individual breeds should be very good. In the United States we tend to have more "all around judges" (those that judge multiple breeds) and use the breeder judges at the specialty shows. Breeder judges are more familiar with their own breed since they are actively breeding that breed or did so at one time. Americans emphasize Group and Best in Show wins and promote them accordingly.

The shows in England can be very large and extend over several days, with the Groups being scheduled on different days. Though multi-day shows are not common in the U.S., there are cluster shows, where several different clubs will use the same show site over consecutive days.

Westminster Kennel Club is our most prestigious show although the entry is limited to 2500. In recent years, entry has

The 1983 Westminster Kennel Club Non-Sporting Group winner was Ch. Lodel's Hijacker of Kralan, owned by Mrs. Nan S. Burke and shown for her by Jack H. Potts.

been limited to Champions. This show is more formal than the majority of the shows with the judges wearing formal attire and the handlers fashionably dressed. In most instances the quality of the dogs is superb. After all, it is a show of Champions. It is a good show to study the AKC registered breeds and is by far the most exciting— especially since it is televised! WKC is one of the few shows in this country that is still benched. This means the dog must be in his benched area during the show hours except when he is being groomed, in the ring, or being exercised.

Ch. Smasher's Pennystone Royal, breeder-owner-handled by Karl Foerster of Kenosha, Wisconsin. Sired by Ch. Smasher's Dan Patch ex Smasher's Encore.

Typically, the handlers are very particular about their appearances. They are careful not to wear something that will detract from their dog but will perhaps enhance it. American ring procedure is quite formal compared to that of other countries. There is a certain etiquette expected between the judge and exhibitor and among the other exhibitors. Of course it is not always the case but the judge is supposed to be polite, not engaging in small talk or acknowledging how well he knows the handler. There is a more informal and relaxed atmosphere at the shows in other countries. For instance, the dress code is more casual. I can see where this might be more fun for the exhibitor and especially for the novice. The U.S. is very handler-oriented in many of the breeds. It is true, in most instances, that the experienced professional handler can present the dog better and will have a feel for what a judge likes, however, most Bulldogs are successfully shown by their owners.

In England, Crufts is The Kennel Club's own show and is most assuredly the largest dog show in the world. They've been known to have an entry of nearly 20,000, and the show lasts four days. Entry is only gained by qualifying through winning in specified classes at another Championship Show. Westminster is strictly conformation, but Crufts exhibitors and spectators enjoy not only conformation but obedience, agility and a multitude of exhibitions as well. Obedience was admitted in 1957 and agility in 1983.

If you are handling your own dog, please give some consideration to your apparel. For sure the dress code at matches is more informal than the point shows. However, you should wear something a little more appropriate than beach attire or ragged jeans and bare feet. If you check out the handlers and see what is presently fashionable, you'll catch on. Men usually dress with a shirt and tie and a nice sports coat. Whether you are male or female, you will want to wear comfortable clothes and shoes. Women usually wear a dress or two-piece outfit, preferably with pockets to carry bait, comb, brush, etc. In this case men are the lucky ones with all their pockets. Ladies, think about where your dress will be if you need to kneel on the floor. Does it allow freedom to do so?

You need to take along dog; crate; ex pen (if you use one); extra newspaper; water pail and water; all required grooming

Eleven-year-old Joshua Estrin with Canadian Ch. Bull Woods Intrepid at the 1981 Chenango Valley Kennel Club Junior Showmanship Competition.

Ch. Sweet Jellyroll Jackson finishing with a five-point major at the Bulldog Club of Northern California Specialty under judge C.D. Richardson. Bred by Bill and Flora Laswell; owner-handled by Fred Zalud.

equipment, table; chair for you; bait for dog and lunch for you and friends; and, last but not least, clean up materials, such as plastic bags, paper towels, and perhaps a bath towel and some shampoo—just in case. Don't forget your entry confirmation and directions to the show.

If you are showing in obedience, then you will want to wear pants. Many of our top obedience handlers wear pants that are color-coordinated with their dogs. The philosophy is that imperfections in the brown dog will be less obvious next to your brown pants.

Whether you are showing in conformation, Junior Showmanship or obedience, you need to watch the clock and be sure you are not late. It is customary to pick up your conformation armband a few minutes before the start of the class. They will not wait for you and if you are on the show grounds and not in the ring, you will upset everyone. It's a little more complicated picking up your obedience armband if you show later in the class. If you have not picked up your armband and they get to your number, you may not be allowed to show. It's best to pick up your armband early, but then you may show earlier than expected if other handlers don't pick up. Customarily all conflicts should be discussed with the judge prior to the start of the class.

Canine Good Citizen

The AKC sponsors a program to encourage dog owners to train their dogs. Local clubs perform the pass/fail tests, and dogs who pass are awarded a Canine Good Citizen Certificate. Proof of vaccination is required at the time of participation. The test includes:

1. Accepting a friendly stranger.
2. Sitting politely for petting.
3. Appearance and grooming.
4. Walking on a loose leash.
5. Walking through a crowd.
6. Sit and down on command/staying in place.
7. Come when called.
8. Reaction to another dog.
9. Reactions to distractions.
10. Supervised separation.

If more effort was made by pet owners to accomplish these exercises, fewer dogs would be cast off to the humane shelter.

Obedience

Obedience is necessary, without a doubt, but it can also become a wonderful hobby or even an obsession. Obedience classes and competition can provide wonderful companionship, not only with your dog but with your classmates or fellow competitors. It is always gratifying to discuss your dog's problems with others who have had similar experiences. The AKC acknowledged Obedience around 1936, and it has changed tremendously even though many of the exercises are basically the same. Today, obedience competition is just that—very competitive. Even so, it is possible for every obedience exhibitor to come home a winner (by

The purpose of the "heel" command is to keep your dog at your side, not pulling in front or lagging behind you. Owner, Frieda McCullough.

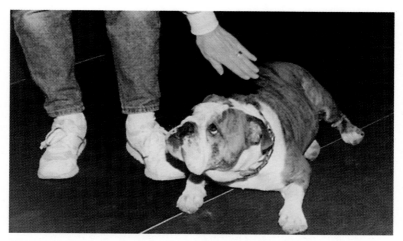

This is Dudley, English Bulldog owned by Frieda McCullough, in the down/stay position.

earning qualifying scores) even though he/she may not earn a placement in the class.

Most of the obedience titles are awarded after earning three qualifying scores (legs) in the appropriate class under three different judges. These classes offer a perfect score of 200, which is extremely rare. Each of the class exercises has its own point value. A leg is earned after receiving a score of at least 170 and at least 50 percent of the points available in each exercise.

TRACKING

Tracking is officially classified obedience. There are three tracking titles available: Tracking Dog (TD), Tracking Dog Excellent (TDX), Variable Surface Tracking (VST). If all three tracking titles are obtained, then the dog officially becomes a CT (Champion Tracker). The CT will go in front of the dog's name.

A TD may be earned anytime and does not have to follow the other obedience titles. There are many exhibitors that prefer tracking to obedience, and there are others who do both.

AGILITY

Agility was first introduced by John Varley in England at the Crufts Dog Show, February 1978, but Peter Meanwell, competitor and judge, actually developed the idea. It was officially recognized in the early '80s. Agility is extremely popular in England and

AKC tracking tests are open to all breeds. Although Bulldogs are not known for having good noses, if given the chance they can enjoy participating in the sport.

Canada and growing in popularity in the U.S. The AKC acknowledged agility in August 1994. Dogs must be at least 12 months of age to be entered. It is a fascinating sport that the dog, handler and spectators enjoy to the utmost. Agility is a spectator sport! The dog performs off lead. The handler either runs with his dog or positions himself on the course and directs his dog with verbal and hand signals over a timed course over or through a variety of obstacles including a time out or pause. One of the main drawbacks to agility is finding a place to train. The obstacles take up a lot of space and it is very time consuming to put up and take down courses.

The titles earned at AKC agility trials are Novice Agility Dog (NAD), Open Agility Dog (OAD), Agility Dog Excellent (ADX), and Master Agility Excellent (MAX). In order to acquire an agility title, a dog must earn a qualifying score in its respective class on three separate occasions under two different judges. The MAX will be awarded after earning ten qualifying scores in the Agility Excellent Class.

GENERAL INFORMATION

Obedience, tracking and agility allow the purebred dog with an Indefinite Listing Privilege (ILP) number or a limited registration to be exhibited and earn titles. Application must be made to the AKC for an ILP number.

The American Kennel Club publishes a monthly *Events* magazine that is part of the *Gazette*, their official journal for the sport of purebred dogs. The *Events* section lists upcoming shows and the secretary or superintendent for them. The majority of the conformation shows in the U.S. are overseen by licensed superintendents. Generally the entry closing date is approximately two-and-a-half weeks before the actual show. Point shows are fairly expensive, while the match shows cost about one third of the point show entry fee. Match shows usually take entries the day of the show but some are pre-entry. The best way to find match show information is through your local kennel club. Upon asking, the AKC can provide you with a list of superintendents, and you can write and ask to be put on their mailing lists.

Obedience trial and tracking test information is available through the AKC. Frequently these events are not superintended, but put on by the host club. Therefore you would make the entry with the event's secretary.

As you have read, there are numerous activities you can share with your dog. Regardless what you do, it does take teamwork. Your dog can only benefit from your attention and training. We hope this chapter has enlightened you and hope, if nothing else, you will attend a show here and there. Perhaps you will start with a puppy kindergarten class, and who knows where it may lead!

BEHAVIOR and Canine Communication

S tudies of the human/animal bond point out the importance of the unique relationships that exist between people and their pets. Those of us who share our lives with pets understand the special part they play through companionship, service and protection. For many, the pet/owner bond goes beyond simple companionship; pets are often considered members of the family. A leading pet food manufacturer recently conducted a nationwide survey of pet owners to gauge just how important pets were in their lives. Here's what they found:

- 76 percent allow their pets to sleep on their beds
- 78 percent think of their pets as their children
- 84 percent display photos of their pets, mostly in their homes
- 84 percent think that their pets react to their own emotions
- 100 percent talk to their pets
- 97 percent think that their pets understand what they're saying
  Are you surprised?

Senior citizens show more concern for their own eating habits when they have the responsibility of feeding a dog. Seeing that their dog is routinely exercised encourages the owner to think of

For many Bulldog owners, the pet/owner bond goes beyond simple companionship; pets are often considered members of the family.

schedules that otherwise may seem unimportant to the senior citizen. The older owner may be arthritic and feeling poorly but with responsibility for his dog he has a reason to get up and get moving. It is a big plus if his dog is an attention seeker who will demand such from his owner.

Over the last couple of decades, it has been shown that pets relieve the stress of those who

Many dog-owning people believe that every child should have the opportunity to have a family dog.

lead busy lives. Owning a pet has been known to lessen the occurrence of heart attack and stroke.

Many single folks thrive on the companionship of a dog. Lifestyles are very different from a long time ago, and today more individuals seek the single life. However, they receive fulfillment from owning a dog.

Most likely the majority of our dogs live in family environments. The companionship they provide is well worth the effort involved. In my opinion, every child should have the opportunity to have a family dog. Dogs teach responsibility through understanding their care, feelings and even respecting their life cycles. Frequently those children who have not been exposed to dogs grow up afraid of dogs, which isn't good. Dogs sense timidity and some will take advantage of the situation.

Today more dogs are serving as service dogs. Since the origination of the Seeing Eye dogs years ago, we now have trained hearing dogs. Also dogs are trained to provide service for the handicapped and are able to perform many different tasks for their owners. Search and Rescue dogs, with their handlers, are sent throughout the world to assist in recovery of disaster victims. They are life savers.

Therapy dogs are very popular with nursing homes, and some hospitals even allow them to visit. The inhabitants truly look

A good breeder tries to place each of his or her Bulldog puppies with the right owners.

forward to their visits. They wanted and were allowed to have visiting dogs in their beds to hold and love.

Nationally there is a Pet Awareness Week to educate students and others about the value and basic care of our pets. Many countries take an even greater interest in their pets than Americans do. In those countries the pets are allowed to accompany their owners into restaurants and shops, etc. In the U.S. this freedom is only available to our service dogs. Even so we think very highly of the human/animal bond.

CANINE BEHAVIOR

Canine behavior problems are the number-one reason for pet owners to dispose of their dogs, either through new homes, humane shelters or euthanasia. Unfortunately there are too many owners who are unwilling to devote the necessary time to properly train their dogs. On the other hand, there are those who not only are concerned about inherited health problems but are also aware of the dog's mental stability.

You may realize that a breed and his group relatives (i.e., sporting, hounds, etc.) show tendencies to behavioral characteristics. An experienced breeder can acquaint you with his breed's personality. Unfortunately many breeds are labeled with poor temperaments when actually the breed as a whole is not affected but only a small percentage of individuals within the breed.

Inheritance and environment contribute to the dog's behavior. Some naïve people suggest inbreeding as the cause of bad temperaments. Inbreeding only results in poor behavior if the ancestors carry the trait. If there are excellent temperaments behind the dogs, then inbreeding will promote good temperaments in the offspring. Did you ever consider that inbreeding is what sets the characteristics of a breed? A purebred dog is the end result of inbreeding. This does not spare the mixed-breed dog from the same problems. Mixed-breed dogs frequently are the offspring of purebred dogs.

Not too many decades ago most of our dogs led a different lifestyle than what is prevalent today. Usually mom stayed home so the dog had human companion-ship and someone to discipline it if needed. Not much was expected from the dog. Today's mom works and everyone's life is at a much faster pace.

The dog may have to adjust to being a "weekend" dog. The family is gone all day during the week, and the dog is left to his own devices for entertainment. Some dogs sleep all day waiting for their family to come home and others become wigwam wreckers if given the opportunity. Crates do ensure the safety of the dog and the house. However, he could become a physically and emotionally cripple if he doesn't get enough exercise and attention. We still appreciate and want the companionship of

Dogs that are left alone all day often become bored, so it makes sense to acquire a pair that will keep each other company while the family is at work or school.

113

our dogs although we expect more from them. In many cases we tend to forget dogs are just that—*dogs* not human beings.

SOCIALIZING AND TRAINING

Many prospective puppy buyers lack experience regarding the proper socialization and training needed to develop the type of pet we all desire. In the first 18 months, training does take some work. It is easier to start proper training before there is a problem that needs to be corrected.

The initial work begins with the breeder. The breeder should start socializing the puppy at five to six weeks of age and cannot let up. Human socializing is critical up through 12 weeks of age and likewise important during the following months. The litter should be left together during the first few weeks but it is necessary to separate them by ten weeks of age. Leaving them together after that time will increase competition for litter dominance. If puppies are not socialized with people by 12 weeks of age, they will be timid in later life.

The eight- to ten-week age period is a fearful time for puppies. They need to be handled very gently around children and adults. There should be no harsh discipline during this time. Starting at 14 weeks of age, the puppy begins the juvenile period, which ends when he reaches sexual maturity around six to 14 months of age. During the juvenile period he needs to be introduced to strangers (adults, children and other dogs) on the home property. At sexual maturity he will begin to bark at strangers and become more protective. Males start to lift their legs to urinate but if you desire you can inhibit this behavior by walking your boy on leash away from trees, shrubs, fences, etc.

Perhaps you are thinking about an older puppy. You need to inquire about the puppy's social experience. If he has lived in a kennel, he may have a hard time adjusting to people and environmental stimuli. Assuming he has had a good social upbringing, there are advantages to an older puppy.

Training includes puppy kindergarten and a minimum of one to two basic training classes. During these classes you will learn how to dominate your youngster. This is especially important if you own a large breed of dog. It is somewhat harder, if not nearly impossible, for some owners to be the Alpha figure when their dog towers over them. You will be taught how to properly restrain your dog. This concept is important. Again it puts you in the Alpha position. All dogs need to be restrained many times during their lives. Believe it or not, some of our worst offenders are the eight-week-old puppies that are brought to our clinic. They need to be gently restrained for a nail trim but the way they carry on you would think we were killing them. In comparison, their vaccination is a "piece of cake." When we ask dogs to do something that is not agreeable to them, then their worst comes out. Life will be easier for your dog if you expose him at a young age to the necessities of life—proper behavior and restraint.

UNDERSTANDING THE DOG'S LANGUAGE

Most authorities agree that the dog is a descendent of the wolf. The dog and wolf have similar traits. For instance both are pack oriented and prefer not to be isolated for long periods of time. Another characteristic is that the dog, like the wolf, looks to the leader—Alpha—for direction. Both the wolf and the dog communicate through body language, not only within their pack but with outsiders.

Every pack has an Alpha figure. The dog looks to you, or should look to you, to be that leader. If your dog doesn't receive the proper training and guidance, he very well may replace you as Alpha. This would be a serious problem and is certainly a disservice to your dog.

Eye contact is one way the Alpha wolf keeps order within his pack. You are Alpha so you must establish eye contact with your puppy. Obviously your puppy will have to look at you. Practice eye contact even if you need to hold his head for five to ten seconds at a time. You can give him a treat as a reward. Make sure your eye contact is gentle and not threatening. Later, if he has been naughty, it is permissible to give him a long, penetrating look. There are some

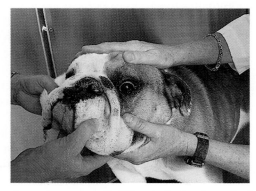

Accustom your Bulldog to being handled from an early age so that visits to the veterinarian are less traumatic for both dog and owner.

older dogs that never learned eye contact as puppies and cannot accept eye contact. You should avoid eye contact with these dogs since they feel threatened and will retaliate as such.

BODY LANGUAGE

The play bow, when the forequarters are down and the hindquarters are elevated, is an invitation to play. Puppies play fight, which helps them learn the acceptable limits of biting. This is necessary for later in their lives. Nevertheless, an owner may be falsely reassured by the playful nature of his dog's aggression. Playful aggression toward another dog or human may be an indication of serious aggression in the future. Owners should never play fight or play tug-of-war with any dog that is inclined to be dominant.

Signs of submission are:

1. Avoids eye contact.
2. Active submission—the dog crouches down, ears back and the tail is lowered.
3. Passive submission—the dog rolls on his side with his hindlegs in the air and frequently urinates.

Signs of dominance are:

1. Makes eye contact.
2. Stands with ears up, tail up and the hair raised on his neck.
3. Shows dominance over another dog by standing at right angles over it.

Dominant dogs tend to behave in characteristic ways such as:

1. The dog may be unwilling to move from his place (i.e., reluctant to give up the sofa if the owner wants to sit there).
2. He may not part with toys or objects in his mouth and may show possessiveness with his food bowl.
3. He may not respond quickly to commands.
4. He may be disagreeable for grooming and dislikes to be petted.

Dogs are popular because of their sociable nature. Those that have contact with humans during the first 12 weeks of life regard them as a member of their own species—their pack. All dogs have the potential for both dominant and submissive behavior. Only through experience and training do they learn to whom it is appropriate to show which behavior. Not all dogs are concerned with dominance but owners need to be aware of that potential. It is wise for the owner to establish his dominance early on.

A human can express dominance or submission toward a dog in the following ways:

1. Meeting the dog's gaze signals dominance. Averting the gaze signals submission. If the dog growls or threatens, averting the gaze is the first avoiding action to take—it may prevent attack. It is important to establish eye contact in the puppy. The older dog that has not been exposed to eye contact may see it as a threat and will not be willing to submit.

2. Being taller than the dog signals dominance; being lower signals submission. This is why, when attempting to make friends with a strange dog or catch the runaway, one should kneel down to his level. Some owners see their dogs become dominant when allowed on the furniture or on the bed. Then he is at the owner's level.

3. An owner can gain dominance by ignoring all the dog's social initiatives. The owner pays attention to the dog only when he obeys a command.

No dog should be allowed to achieve dominant status over any adult or child. Ways of preventing are as follows:

1. Handle the puppy gently, especially during the three- to four-month period.

2. Let the children and adults handfeed him and teach him to take food without lunging or grabbing.

3. Do not allow him to chase children or joggers.

Only through experience and training do dogs learn appropriate behavior.

4. Do not allow him to jump on people or mount their legs. Even females may be inclined to mount. It is not only a male habit.

5. Do not allow him to growl for any reason.

6. Don't participate in wrestling or tug-of-war games.

7. Don't physically punish puppies for aggressive behavior. Restrain him from repeating the infraction and teach an alternative behavior. Dogs should earn everything they receive from their owners. This would include sitting to receive petting or treats, sitting before going out the door and sitting to receive the collar and leash. These types of exercises reinforce the owner's dominance.

Young children should never be left alone with a dog. It is important that children learn some basic obedience commands so they have some control over the dog. They will gain the respect of their dog.

FEAR

One of the most common problems dogs experience is being fearful. Some dogs are more afraid than others. On the lesser side,

Always supervise your Bulldog and child when they are playing with each other.

which is sometimes humorous to watch, dogs can be afraid of a strange object. They act silly when something is out of place in the house. We call his problem perceptive intelligence. He realizes the abnormal within his known environment. He does not react the same way in strange environments since he does not know what is normal.

On the more serious side is a fear of people. This can result in backing off, seeking his own space and saying "leave me alone" or it can result in an aggressive behavior that may lead to *No puppy should be permitted to achieve dominant status over any adult or child.*

challenging the person. Respect that the dog wants to be left alone and give him time to come forward. If you approach the cornered dog, he may resort to snapping. If you leave him alone, he may decide to come forward, which should be rewarded with a treat.

Some dogs may initially be too fearful to take treats. In these cases it is helpful to make sure the dog hasn't eaten for about 24 hours. Being a little hungry encourages him to accept the treats, especially if they are of the "gourmet" variety.

Dogs can be afraid of numerous things, including loud noises and thunderstorms. Invariably the owner rewards (by comforting) the dog when it shows signs of fearfulness. When your dog is frightened, direct his attention to something else and act happy. Don't dwell on his fright.

AGGRESSION

Some different types of aggression are: predatory, defensive, dominance, possessive, protective, fear induced, noise provoked, "rage" syndrome (unprovoked aggression), maternal and aggression directed toward other dogs. Aggression is the most common behavioral problem encountered. Protective breeds are expected to be more aggressive than others but with the proper upbringing they can make very dependable companions. You need to be able to read your dog.

Many factors contribute to aggression including genetics and environment. An improper environment, which may include the living conditions, lack of social life, excessive punishment, being attacked or frightened by an aggressive dog, etc., can all influence a dog's behavior. Even spoiling him and giving too much praise may be detrimental. Isolation and the lack of human contact or exposure to frequent teasing by children or adults also can ruin a good dog.

Lack of direction, fear, or confusion lead to aggression in those dogs that are so inclined. Any obedience exercise, even the sit and down, can direct the dog and overcome fear and/or confusion.

Tug toys are famous for causing aggressive behavior in dogs. It is best to avoid engaging in games of this type with your Bulldog.

It may seem as though a Bulldog's outlook on life is extremely serious, but the breed actually does have a terrific sense of humor.

Every dog should learn these commands as a youngster, and there should be periodic reinforcement.

When a dog is showing signs of aggression, you should speak calmly (no screaming or hysterics) and firmly give a command that he understands, such as the sit. As soon as your dog obeys, you have assumed your dominant position. Aggression presents a problem because there may be danger to others. Sometimes it is an emotional issue. Owners may consciously or unconsciously encourage their dog's aggression. Other owners show responsibility by accepting the problem and taking measures to keep it under control. The owner is responsible for his dog's actions, and it is not wise to take a chance on someone being bitten, especially a child. Euthanasia is the solution for some owners and in severe cases this may be the best choice. However, few dogs are that dangerous and very few are that much of a threat to their owners. If caution is exercised and professional help is gained early on, most cases can be controlled.

Some authorities recommend feeding a lower protein (less than 20 percent) diet. They believe this can aid in reducing aggression. If the dog loses weight, then vegetable oil can be added. Veterinarians and behaviorists are having some success with pharmacology. In many cases treatment is possible and can improve the situation.

If you have done everything according to "the book" regarding training and socializing and are still having a behavior problem, don't procrastinate. It is important that the problem gets attention before it is out of hand. It is estimated that 20 percent of a veterinarian's time may be devoted to dealing with problems before they become so intolerable that the dog is separated from its home and owner. If your veterinarian isn't able to help, he should refer you to a behaviorist.

PROBLEMS

Barking

This is a habit that shouldn't be encouraged. Some owners desire their dog to bark so as to be a watchdog. Most dogs will bark when a stranger comes to the door.

The new puppy frequently barks or whines in the crate in his strange environment and the owner reinforces the puppy's bad behavior by going to him during the night. This is a no-no.

Smack the top of the crate and say "quiet" in a loud, firm voice. The puppies don't like to hear the loud noise of the crate being banged. If the barking is sleep-interrupting, then the owner should take crate and pup to the bedroom for a few days until the puppy becomes adjusted to his new environment. Otherwise ignore the barking during the night.

A well-mannered Bulldog will be a joy to own and to live near. Do not allow your Bulldog to bark while outdoors—your neighbors will certainly not appreciate it.

Barking can be an inherited problem or a bad habit learned through the environment. It takes dedication to stop the barking. Attention should be paid to the cause of the barking. Does the dog seek attention, does he need to go out, is it feeding time, is it occurring when he is left alone, is it a protective bark, etc.? Overzealous barking is an inherited tendency. When barking presents a problem for you, try to stop it as soon as it begins.

There are elecronic collars available that are supposed to curb barking. There are some disadvantages to to the collar. If the dog is barking out of excitement, punish-ment is not the appropriate treatment. Presumably there is the chance the collar could be activated by other stimuli and thereby punish the dog when it is not barking. Should you decide to use one, then you should seek help from a person with experience with that type of collar. Nevertheless the root of the problem needs to be investigated and corrected.

Jumping Up

A dog that jumps up is a happy dog. Nevertheless few guests appreciate dogs jumping on them. Clothes get footprinted and/or snagged.

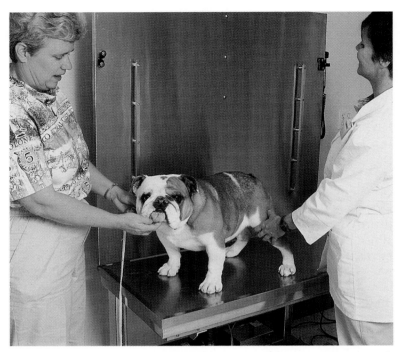

If your Bulldog is displaying behavior problems, you may seek help through your veterinarian, dog trainer, and/or behaviorist.

Some trainers believe in allowing the puppy to jump up during his first few weeks. If you correct him too soon and at the wrong age you may intimidate him. Consequently he could be timid around humans later in his life. However, there will come a time, probably around four months of age, that he needs to know when it is okay to jump and when he is to show off good manners by sitting instead.

Some authorities never allow jumping. If you are irritated by your dog jumping up on you, then you should discourage it from the beginning. A larger breed of dog can cause harm to a senior citizen. Some are quite fragile. It may not take much to cause a topple that could break a hip.

How do you correct the problem? All family members need to participate in teaching the puppy to sit as soon as he starts to jump up. The sit must be practiced every time he starts to jump up. Don't forget to praise him for his good behavior. If an older dog has acquired the habit, grasp his paws and squeeze tightly. Give a firm "No." He'll soon catch on. Remember the entire family must take part. Each time you allow him to jump up you go back a step in training.

Biting

All puppies bite and try to chew on your fingers, toes, arms, etc. This is the time to teach them to be gentle and not bite hard. Put your fingers in your puppy's mouth and if he bites too hard then say "easy" and let him know he's hurting you. Squeal and act like you have been seriously hurt. If the puppy plays too rough and doesn't respond to your corrections, then he needs "Time Out" in his crate. You should be particularly careful with young children and puppies who still have their deciduous (baby) teeth. Those teeth are like needles and can leave little scars on youngsters.

Biting in the more mature dog is something that should be prevented at all costs. Should it occur quickly let him know in no uncertain terms that biting will not be tolerated. When biting is directed toward another dog (dog fight), don't get in the middle of it. Some authorities recommend breaking up a fight by elevating the hind legs. This would only be possible if there was a person for each dog. Obviously it would be hard to fight with the hind legs off the ground. A dog bite is serious and should be given attention. Wash the bite with soap and water and contact your doctor. It is important to know the status of the offender's rabies vaccination.

Your dog must know who is boss. When biting occurs, you should seek professional help at once. On the other hand you must not let your dog intimidate you and be so afraid of a bite that you can't discipline him. Professional help through your veterinarian, dog trainer and/or behaviorist can give you guidance.

HEALTH CARE

Veterinary medicine has become far more sophisticated than what was available to our ancestors. This can be attributed to the increase in household pets and consequently the demand for better care for them. Also human medicine has become far more complex. Today diagnostic testing in veterinary medicine parallels human diagnostics. Because of better technology we can expect our pets to live healthier lives thereby increasing their life spans.

THE FIRST CHECK UP

You will want to take your new puppy/dog in for its first check up within 48 to 72 hours after acquiring it. Many breeders strongly recommend this check up and so do the humane shelters. A puppy/dog can appear healthy but it may have a serious problem that is not apparent to the layman. Most pets have some type of a minor flaw that may never cause a real problem.

Unfortunately if he/she should have a serious problem, you will want to consider the consequences of keeping the pet and the attachments that will be formed, which may be broken prematurely. Keep in mind there are many healthy dogs looking for good homes.

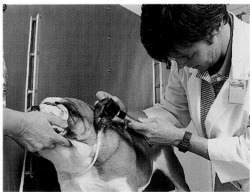

This first check up is a good time to establish yourself with the veterinarian and learn the office policy regarding their hours and how they handle emergencies. Usually the breeder or another conscientious pet owner is a good reference for locating a capable veterinarian. You should be aware that not all veterinarians give the same quality of service.

Next to you, your veterinarian will be your Bulldog's best friend. It is important that you and your pet develop a good relationship with the doctor so that visits are more pleasurable.

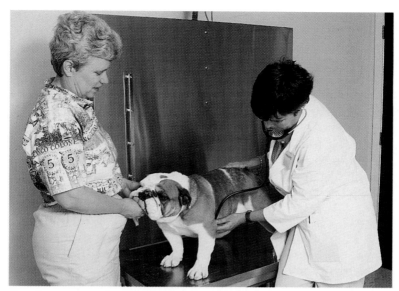

During annual examinations by your veterinarian, your Bulldog will have his ears, teeth, and heart checked, as well as receive booster shots.

Please do not make your selection on the least expensive clinic, as they may be short changing your pet. There is the possibility that eventually it will cost you more due to improper diagnosis, treatment, etc. If you are selecting a new veterinarian, feel free to ask for a tour of the clinic. You should inquire about making an appointment for a tour since all clinics are working clinics, and therefore may not be available all day for sightseers. You may worry less if you see where your pet will be spending the day if he ever needs to be hospitalized.

THE PHYSICAL EXAM

Your veterinarian will check your pet's overall condition, which includes listening to the heart; checking the respiration; feeling the abdomen, muscles and joints; checking the mouth, which includes the gum color and signs of gum disease along with plaque buildup; checking the ears for signs of an infection or ear mites; examining the eyes; and, last but not least, checking the condition of the skin and coat.

He should ask you questions regarding your pet's eating and elimination habits and invite you to relay your questions. It is a good idea to prepare a list so as not to forget anything. He should discuss the proper diet and the quantity to be fed. If this should differ from your breeder's recommendation, then you should convey to him the breeder's choice and see if he approves. If he recommends changing the diet, then this should be done over a few days so as not to cause a gastrointestinal upset. It is customary to take in a fresh stool sample (just a small amount) for a test for intestinal parasites. It must be fresh, preferably within 12 hours, since the eggs hatch quickly and after hatching will not be observed under the microscope. If your pet isn't obliging then, usually the technician can take one in the clinic.

IMMUNIZATIONS

It is important that you take your puppy/dog's vaccination record with you on your first visit. In case of a puppy, presumably the breeder has seen to the vaccinations up to the time you acquired custody. Veterinarians differ in their vaccination protocol. It is not unusual for your puppy to have received vaccinations for distemper, hepatitis, leptospirosis, parvovirus and parainfluenza every two to three weeks from the age of five or six weeks. Usually this is a combined injection and is typically called the DHLPP. The DHLPP is given through at least 12 to 14 weeks of age, and it is customary to continue with another parvovirus vaccine at 16 to 18 weeks. You may wonder why so many immunizations are

Puppies should not leave the breeder's premises without having had at least one set of puppy shots.

necessary. No one knows for sure when the puppy's maternal antibodies are gone, although it is customarily accepted that distemper antibodies are gone by 12 weeks. Usually parvovirus antibodies are gone by 16 to 18 weeks of age. However, it is possible for the maternal antibodies to be gone at a much earlier age or even a later age. Therefore immunizations are started at an early age. The vaccine will not give immunity as long as there are maternal antibodies.

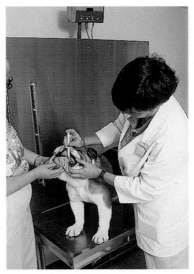

Vaccinations will help immunize your dog against contagious disease.

The rabies vaccination is given at three or six months of age depending on your local laws. A vaccine for bordetella (kennel cough) is advisable and can be given anytime from the age of five weeks. The coronavirus is not commonly given unless there is a problem locally. The Lyme vaccine is necessary in endemic areas. Lyme disease has been reported in 47 states.

Distemper

This is virtually an incurable disease. If the dog recovers, he is subject to severe nervous disorders. The virus attacks every tissue in the body and resembles a bad cold with a fever. It can cause a runny nose and eyes and cause gastrointestinal disorders, including a poor appetite, vomiting and diarrhea. The virus is carried by raccoons, foxes, wolves, mink and other dogs. Unvaccinated youngsters and senior citizens are very susceptible. This is still a common disease.

Hepatitis

This is a virus that is most serious in very young dogs. It is spread by contact with an infected animal or its stool or urine. The virus affects the liver and kidneys and is characterized by high fever, depression and lack of appetite. Recovered animals may be afflicted with chronic illnesses.

Leptospirosis

This is a bacterial disease transmitted by contact with the urine of an infected dog, rat or other wildlife. It produces severe symptoms of fever, depression, jaundice and internal bleeding and was fatal before the vaccine was developed. Recovered dogs can be carriers, and the disease can be transmitted from dogs to humans.

Parvovirus

This was first noted in the late 1970s and is still a fatal disease. However, with proper vaccinations, early diagnosis and prompt treatment, it is a manageable disease. It attacks the bone marrow and intestinal tract. The symptoms include depression, loss of appetite, vomiting, diarrhea and collapse. Immediate medical attention is of the essence.

Rabies

This is shed in the saliva and is carried by raccoons, skunks, foxes, other dogs and cats. It attacks nerve tissue, resulting in paralysis and death. Rabies can be transmitted to people and is virtually always fatal. This disease is reappearing in the suburbs.

Bordetella (Kennel Cough)

The symptoms are coughing, sneezing, hacking and retching accompanied by nasal discharge usually lasting from a few days to

Many potential dangers hide in the great outdoors. Always supervise your Bulldog while he is outside and thoroughly check him for fleas and ticks before he comes in.

An annual visit to the veterinarian will keep potential problems from becoming serious.

several weeks. There are several disease-producing organisms responsible for this disease. The present vaccines are helpful but do not protect for all the strains. It usually is not life threatening but in some instances it can progress to a serious bronchopneumonia. The disease is highly contagious. The vaccination should be given routinely for dogs that come in contact with other dogs, such as through boarding, training class or visits to the groomer.

Coronavirus

This is usually self limiting and not life threatening. It was first noted in the late 70s about a year before parvovirus. The virus produces a yellow/brown stool and there may be depression, vomiting and diarrhea.

Lyme Disease

This was first diagnosed in the United States in 1976 in Lyme, CT in people who lived in close proximity to the deer tick. Symptoms may include acute lameness, fever, swelling of joints and loss of appetite. Your veterinarian can advise you if you live in an endemic area.

After your puppy has completed his puppy vaccinations, you will continue to booster the DHLPP once a year. It is customary to booster the rabies one year after the first vaccine and then, depending on where you live, it should be boostered every year or every three years. This depends on your local laws. The Lyme and corona vaccines are boostered annually and it is recommended that the bordetella be boostered every six to eight months.

ANNUAL VISIT

I would like to impress the importance of the annual check up, which would include the booster vaccinations, check for intestinal parasites and test for heartworm. Today in our very busy world it is rush, rush and see "how much you can get for how little." Unbelievably, some non-veterinary businesses have entered into the vaccination business. More harm than good can come to your dog through improper vaccinations, possibly from inferior vaccines and/or the wrong schedule. More than likely you truly care about your companion dog and over the years you have devoted much time and expense to his well being. Perhaps you are unaware that a vaccination is not just a vaccination. There is more involved. Please, please follow through with regular physical examinations. It is so important for your veterinarian to know your dog and this is especially true during middle age through the geriatric years. More than likely your older dog will require more than one physical a year. The annual physical is good preventive medicine. Through early diagnosis and subsequent treatment your dog can maintain a longer and better quality of life.

INTESTINAL PARASITES

Hookworms

These are almost microscopic intestinal worms that can cause anemia and therefore serious problems, including death, in young puppies. Hookworms can be transmitted to humans through penetration of the skin. Puppies may be born with them.

Roundworms

These are spaghetti-like worms that can cause a potbellied appearance and dull coat along with more severe symptoms, such as vomiting, diarrhea and coughing. Puppies acquire these while in the mother's uterus and through lactation. Both hookworms and roundworms may be acquired through ingestion.

Whipworms

These have a three-month life cycle and are not acquired through the dam. They cause intermittent diarrhea usually with mucus. Whipworms are possibly the most difficult worm to eradicate. Their eggs are very resistant to most environmental factors and can last for years until the proper conditions enable them to mature. Whipworms are seldom seen in the stool.

Intestinal parasites are more prevalent in some areas than others. Climate, soil and contamination are big factors contributing to the incidence of intestinal parasites. Eggs are passed in the stool, lay on the ground and then become infective in a certain number of days. Each of the above worms has a different life cycle. Your best chance of becoming and remaining worm-free is to always pooper-scoop your yard. A fenced-in yard keeps stray dogs out, which is certainly helpful.

I would recommend having a fecal examination on your dog twice a year or more often if there is a problem. If your dog has a positive fecal sample, then he will be given the appropriate medication and you will be asked to bring back another stool sample in a certain period of time (depending on the type of worm) and then be rewormed. This process goes on until he has at least two negative samples. The different types of worms require different medications. You will be wasting your money and doing your dog an injustice by buying over-the-counter medication without first consulting your veterinarian.

Adult whipworms. These are possibly the most difficult worm to eradicate.

Coccidiosis and Giardiasis

These protozoal infections usually affect puppies, especially in places where large numbers of puppies are brought together. Older dogs may harbor these infections but do not show signs unless they are stressed. Symptoms include diarrhea, weight loss and lack of appetite. These infections are not always apparent in the fecal examination.

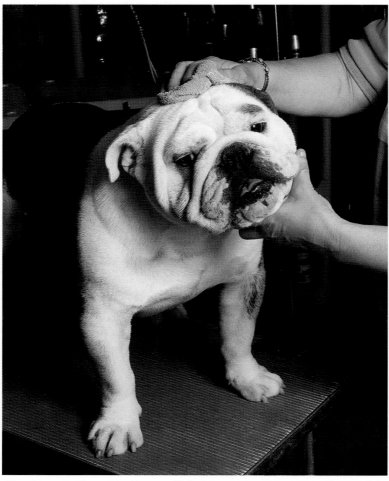

Good grooming practices will help you keep on top of any skin conditions your dog may have.

Tapeworms

Seldom apparent on fecal floatation, they are diagnosed frequently as rice-like segments around the dog's anus and the base of the tail. Tapeworms are long, flat and ribbon like, sometimes several feet in length, and made up of many segments about five-eighths of an inch long. The two most common types of tapeworms found in the dog are:

(1) First the larval form of the flea tapeworm parasite must mature in an intermediate host, the flea, before it can become infective. Your dog acquires this by ingesting the flea through licking and chewing.

(2) Rabbits, rodents and certain large game animals serve as intermediate hosts for other species of tapeworms. If your dog should eat one of these infected hosts, then he can acquire tapeworms.

HEARTWORM DISEASE

This is a worm that resides in the heart and adjacent blood vessels of the lung that produces microfilaria, which circulate in the bloodstream. It is possible for a dog to be infected with any number of worms from one to a hundred that can be 6 to 14 inches long. It is a life-threatening disease, expensive to treat and easily prevented. Depending on where you live, your veterinarian may recommend a preventive year-round and either an annual or semiannual blood test. The most common preventive is given once a month.

EXTERNAL PARASITES

Fleas

These pests are not only the dog's worst enemy but also enemy to the owner's pocketbook. Preventing is less expensive than treating, but regardless we'd prefer to spend our money elsewhere. Likely, the majority of our dogs are allergic to the bite of a flea, and in many cases it only takes one flea bite. The protein in the flea's saliva is the culprit. Allergic dogs have a reaction, which usually results in a "hot spot." More than likely such a reaction will involve a trip to the veterinarian for treatment. Yes, prevention is less expensive. Fortunately today there are several good products available.

If there is a flea infestation, no one product is going to correct the problem. Not only will the dog require treatment so will the environment. In general flea collars are not very effective although there is now available an "egg" collar that will kill the eggs on the dog. Dips are the most economical but they are messy. There are some effective shampoos and treatments available through pet shops and veterinarians. An oral tablet arrived on the American market in 1995 and was popular in Europe the previous year. It sterilizes the female flea but will not kill adult fleas. Therefore the tablet, which is given monthly, will decrease the flea population but is not a "cure-all." Those dogs that suffer from flea-bite allergy will still be subjected to the bite of the flea. Another popular parasiticide is permethrin, which is applied to the back of the dog in one or two places depending on the dog's weight. This product works as a repellent causing the flea to get "hot feet" and jump off. Do not confuse this product with some of the organophosphates that are also applied to the dog's back.

Some products are not usable on young puppies. Treating fleas should be done under your veterinarian's guidance. Frequently it is necessary to combine products and the layman does not have the knowledge regarding possible toxicities. It is hard to believe but there are a few dogs that do have a natural resistance to fleas.

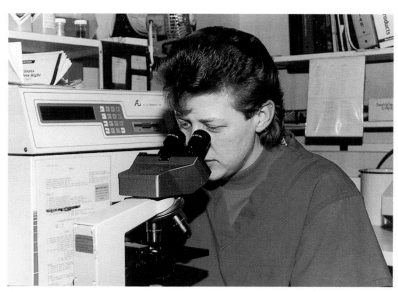

Laboratory tests are studied by highly trained veterinary technicians. Most tests are performed right in your veterinarian's office and results are usually available the same day.

Check your Bulldog's coat thoroughly for any parasites, especially after playing outdoors.

Nevertheless it would be wise to treat all pets at the same time. Don't forget your cats. Cats just love to prowl the neighborhood and consequently return with unwanted guests.

Adult fleas live on the dog but their eggs drop off the dog into the environment. There they go through four larval stages before reaching adulthood, and thereby are able to jump back on the poor unsuspecting dog. The cycle resumes and takes between 21 to 28 days under ideal conditions. There are environmental products available that will kill both the adult fleas and the larvae.

Ticks

Ticks carry Rocky Mountain Spotted Fever, Lyme disease and can cause tick paralysis. They should be removed with tweezers, trying to pull out the head. The jaws carry disease. There is a tick preventive collar that does an excellent job. The ticks automatically back out on those dogs wearing collars.

Sarcoptic Mange

This is a mite that is difficult to find on skin scrapings. The pinnal reflex is a good indicator of this disease. Rub the ends of the pinna (ear) together and the dog will start scratching with his foot. Sarcoptes are highly contagious to other dogs and to humans although they do not live long on humans. They cause intense itching.

Demodectic Mange

This is a mite that is passed from the dam to her puppies. It affects youngsters age three to ten months. Diagnosis is confirmed by skin scraping. Small areas of alopecia around the eyes, lips and/ or forelegs become visible. There is little itching unless there is a secondary bacterial infection. Some breeds are afflicted more than others.

Cheyletiella

This causes intense itching and is diagnosed by skin scraping. It lives in the outer layers of the skin of dogs, cats, rabbits and humans. Yellow-gray scales may be found on the back and the rump, top of the head and the nose.

Newborn pups with their mother. At this stage, their only concerns in life are keeping warm and eating.

To Breed or Not To Breed

More than likely your breeder has requested that you have your puppy neutered or spayed. Your breeder's request is based on what is healthiest for your dog and what is most beneficial for your breed. Experienced and conscientious breeders devote many years

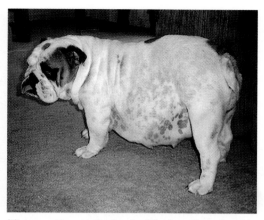

This mother-to-be looks like her "big day" is only moments away.

into developing a bloodline. In order to do this, he makes every effort to plan each breeding in regard to conformation, temperament and health. This type of breeder does his best to perform the necessary testing (i.e., OFA, CERF, testing for inherited blood disorders, thyroid, etc.). Testing is expensive and sometimes very disheartening when a favorite dog doesn't pass his health tests. The health history pertains not only to the breeding stock but to the immediate ancestors. Reputable breeders do not want their offspring to be bred indiscriminately. Therefore you may be asked to neuter or spay your puppy. Of course there is always the exception, and your breeder may agree to let you breed your dog under his direct supervision. This is an important concept. More and more effort is being made to breed healthier dogs.

Spay/Neuter

There are numerous benefits of performing this surgery at six months of age. Unspayed females are subject to mammary and ovarian cancer. In order to prevent mammary cancer she must be spayed prior to her first heat cycle. Later in life, an unspayed female may develop a pyometra (an infected uterus), which is definitely life threatening.

Spaying is performed under a general anesthetic and is easy on the young dog. As you might expect it is a little harder on the older dog, but that is no reason to deny her the surgery. The surgery removes the ovaries and uterus. It is important to remove all the

Breeding should only be attempted by someone who is conscientious, knowledgeable, and willing to take responsibility for the dogs and the new puppies involved.

ovarian tissue. If some is left behind, she could remain attractive to males. In order to view the ovaries, a reasonably long incision is necessary. An ovariohysterectomy is considered major surgery.

Neutering the male at a young age will inhibit some characteristic male behavior that owners frown upon. Some boys will not hike their legs and mark territory if they are neutered at six months of age. Also neutering at a young age has hormonal benefits, lessening the chance of hormonal aggressiveness.

Surgery involves removing the testicles but leaving the scrotum. If there should be a retained testicle, then he definitely needs to be neutered before the age of two or three years. Retained testicles can develop into cancer. Unneutered males are at risk for testicular cancer, perineal fistulas, perianal tumors and fistulas and prostatic disease.

Intact males and females are prone to housebreaking accidents. Females urinate frequently before, during and after heat cycles, and males tend to mark territory if there is a female in heat. Males may show the same behavior if there is a visiting dog or guests.

Surgery involves a sterile operating procedure equivalent to human surgery. The incision site is shaved, surgically scrubbed and draped. The veterinarian wears a sterile surgical gown, cap, mask and gloves. Anesthesia should be monitored by a registered technician. It is customary for the veterinarian to recommend a pre-anesthetic blood screening, looking for metabolic problems and a ECG rhythm strip to check for normal heart function. Today anesthetics are equal to human anesthetics, which enables your dog to walk out of the clinic the same day as surgery.

Some folks worry about their dog gaining weight after being neutered or spayed. This is usually not the case. It is true that some dogs may be less active so they could develop a problem, but most dogs are just as active as they were before surgery. However, if your dog should begin to gain, then you need to decrease his food and see to it that he gets a little more exercise.

DENTAL CARE for Your Dog's Life

So you've got a new puppy! You also have a new set of puppy teeth in your household. Anyone who has ever raised a puppy is abundantly aware of these new teeth. Your puppy will chew anything it can reach, chase your shoelaces, and play "tear the rag" with any piece of clothing it can find. When puppies are newly born, they have no teeth. At about four weeks of age, puppies of most breeds begin to develop their deciduous or baby teeth. They begin eating semi-solid food, fighting and biting with their litter mates, and learning discipline from their mother. As their new teeth come in, they

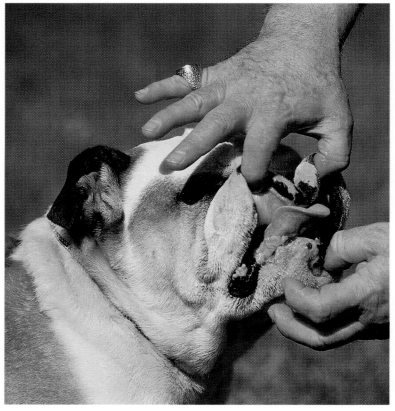

If your train your Bulldog to have good chewing habits as a puppy, he will have healthy teeth throughout his lifetime.

Puppies will chew just about anything they can get their paws on, so provide them with plenty of safe Nylabone® products.

inflict more pain on their mother's breasts, so her feeding sessions become less frequent and shorter. By six or eight weeks, the mother will start growling to warn her pups when they are fighting too roughly or hurting her as they nurse too much with their new teeth.

Puppies need to chew. It is a necessary part of their physical and mental development. They develop muscles and necessary life skills as they drag objects around, fight over possession, and vocalize alerts and warnings. Puppies chew on things to explore their world. They are using their sense of taste to determine what is food and what is not. How else can they tell an electrical cord from a lizard? At about four months of age, most puppies begin shedding their baby teeth. Often these teeth need some help to come out and make way for the permanent teeth. The incisors (front teeth) will be replaced first. Then, the adult canine or fang teeth erupt. When the baby tooth is not shed before the permanent tooth comes in, veterinarians call it a retained deciduous tooth.

This condition will often cause gum infections by trapping hair and debris between the permanent tooth and the retained baby tooth. Nylafloss® is an excellent device for puppies to use. They can toss it, drag it, and chew on the many surfaces it presents. The baby teeth can catch in the nylon material, aiding in their removal. Puppies that have adequate chew toys will have less destructive behavior, develop more physically, and have less chance of retained deciduous teeth.

During the first year, your dog should be seen by your veterinarian at regular intervals. Your veterinarian will let you know when to bring in your puppy for vaccinations and parasite examinations. At each visit, your veterinarian should inspect the lips, teeth, and mouth as part of a complete physical examination. You should take some part in the maintenance of your dog's oral health. You should examine your dog's mouth weekly throughout his first year to make sure there are no sores, foreign objects, tooth problems, etc. If your dog drools excessively, shakes its head, or has bad breath, consult your veterinarian. By the time your dog is six months old, the permanent teeth are all in and plaque can start to accumulate on the tooth surfaces. This is when your dog needs

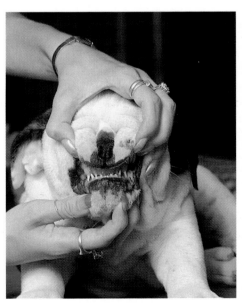

A thorough oral inspection should be a part of your dog's regular physical exam.

to develop good dental-care habits to prevent calculus build-up on its teeth. Brushing is best. That is a fact that cannot be denied. However, some dogs do not like their teeth brushed regularly, or you may not be able to accomplish the task. In that case, you should consider a product that will help prevent plaque and calculus build-up.

A super option for your dog is the Hercules Bone®, a uniquely shaped bone named after the great Olympian

All dogs need to chew. Chew toys like Nylabones® will keep both your dog and your belongings safe.

Olympian for its exception strength. Like all Nylabone products, they are specially scented to make them attractive to your dog. Ask your veterinarian about these bones and he will validate the good doctor's prescription: Nylabones® not only give your dog a good chewing workout but also help to save your dog's teeth (and even his life, as it protects him from possible fatal periodontal diseases).

By the time dogs are four years old, 75% of them have periodontal disease. It is the most common infection in dogs. Yearly examinations by your veterinarian are essential to maintaining your dog's good health. If your veterinarian detects periodontal disease, he or she may recommend a prophylactic cleaning. To do a thorough cleaning, it will be necessary to put your dog under anesthesia. With modern gas anesthetics and monitoring equipment, the procedure is pretty safe. Your veterinarian will scale the teeth with an ultrasound scaler or

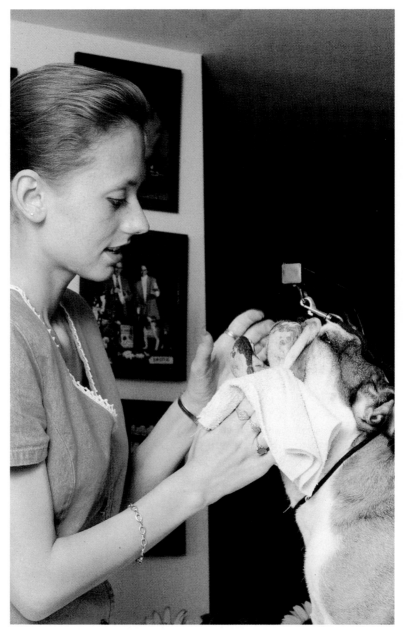

An oral examination should be a part of your Bulldog's annual checkup.

hand instrument. This removes the calculus from the teeth. If there are calculus deposits below the gum line, the veterinarian will plane the roots to make them smooth. After all of the calculus has been removed, the teeth are polished with pumice in a polishing cup. If any medical or surgical treatment is needed, it is done at this time. The final step would be fluoride treatment and your follow-up treatment at home. If the periodontal disease is advanced, the veterinarian may prescribe a medicated mouth rinse or antibiotics for use at home. Make sure your dog has safe, clean and attractive chew toys and treats. Chooz® treats are another way of using a consumable treat to help keep your dog's teeth clean.

As your dog ages, professional examination and cleaning should become more frequent. The mouth should be inspected at least once a year. Your veterinarian may recommend visits every six months. In the geriatric patient, organs such as the heart, liver, and kidneys do not function as well as when they were young. Your veterinarian will probably want to test these organs' functions prior to using general anesthesia for dental cleaning. If your dog is a good chewer and you work closely with your veterinarian, your dog can keep all of its teeth all of its life. However, as your dog ages, his sense of smell, sight, and taste will diminish. He may not have the desire to chase, trap or chew his toys. He will also not have the energy to chew for long periods, as arthritis and periodontal disease make chewing painful. This will leave you with more responsibility for keeping his teeth clean and healthy. The dog that would not let you brush his teeth at one year of age, may let you brush his teeth now that he is ten years old.

If you train your dog with good chewing habits as a puppy, he will have healthier teeth throughout his life.

IDENTIFICATION and Finding the Lost Dog

There are several ways of identifying your dog. The old standby is a collar with dog license, rabies, and ID tags. Unfortunately collars have a way of being separated from the dog and tags fall off. We're not suggesting you shouldn't use a collar and tags. If they stay intact and on the dog, they are the quickest way of identification.

For several years owners have been tattooing their dogs. Some tattoos use a number with a registry. Here lies the problem because there are several registries to check. If you wish to tattoo, use your social security number. The humane shelters have the means to trace it. It is usually done on the inside of the rear thigh. The area is first shaved and numbed. There is no pain, although a few dogs do not like the buzzing sound. Occasionally tattooing is not legible and needs to be redone.

The newest method of identification is microchipping. The microchip is a computer chip that is no larger than a grain of rice. The veterinarian implants it by injection between the shoulder blades. The dog feels no discomfort. If your dog is lost and picked up by the humane society, they can trace you by scanning the

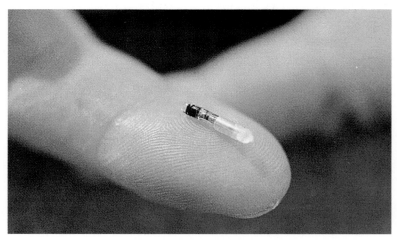

The AKC Companion Animal Recovery Program registers both tattoo numbers and microchip identification information about your pet.

148

Deciding between these two charmers is certainly a difficult choice and breeder Dewey Ritter found it no less difficult.

microchip, which has its own code. Microchip scanners are friendly to other brands of microchips and their registries. The microchip comes with a dog tag saying the dog is microchipped. It is the safest way of identifying your dog.

FINDING THE LOST DOG

I am sure you will agree that there would be little worse than losing your dog. Responsible pet owners rarely lose their dogs. They do not let their dogs run free because they don't want harm to come to them. Not only that but in most, if not all, states there is a leash law.

Beware of fenced-in yards. They can be a hazard. Dogs find ways to escape either over or under the fence. Another fast exit is through the gate that perhaps the neighbor's child left unlocked.

Below is a list that hopefully will be of help to you if you need it. Remember don't give up, keep looking. Your dog is worth your efforts.

1. Contact your neighbors and put flyers with a photo on it in their mailboxes. Information you should include would be the dog's name, breed, sex, color, age, source of identification, when your dog was last seen and where, and your name and phone numbers. It may be helpful to say the dog needs medical care. Offer a *reward*.

2. Check all local shelters daily. It is also possible for your dog to be picked up away from home and end up in an out-of-the-way shelter. Check these too. Go in person. It is not good enough to call. Most shelters are limited on the time they can hold dogs then they are put up for adoption or euthanized. There is the possibility that your dog will not make it to the shelter for several days. Your dog could have been wandering or someone may have tried to keep him.

3. Notify all local veterinarians. Call and send flyers.

4. Call your breeder. Frequently breeders are contacted when one of their breed is found.

5. Contact the rescue group for your breed.

6. Contact local schools—children may have seen your dog.

7. Post flyers at the schools, groceries, gas stations, convenience stores, veterinary clinics, groomers and any other place that will allow them.

8. Advertise in the newspaper.

9. Advertise on the radio.

Mij Charbonneau's "Budkis" has all his gear in line and is completely ready for team tryouts.

TRAVELING with Your Dog

The earlier you start traveling with your new puppy or dog, the better. He needs to become accustomed to traveling. However, some dogs are nervous riders and become carsick easily. It is helpful if he starts with an empty stomach. Do not despair, as it will go better if you continue taking him with you on short fun rides. How would you feel if every time you rode in the car you stopped at the doctor's for an injection? You would soon dread that nasty car. Older dogs that tend to get carsick may have more of a problem adjusting to traveling. Those dogs that are having a serious problem may benefit from some medication prescribed by the veterinarian.

Do give your dog a chance to relieve himself before getting into the car. It is a good idea to be prepared for a clean up with a leash, paper towels, bag and terry cloth towel.

The safest place for your dog is in a fiberglass crate, although close confinement can promote carsickness in some dogs. If your dog is nervous you can try letting him ride on the seat next to you or in someone's lap.

An alternative to the crate would be to use a car harness made for dogs and/or a safety strap attached to the harness or collar. Whatever you do, do not let your dog ride in the back of a pickup

Never allow your Bulldog to stick his head out of an open window while the car is moving as foreign debris can blow into his eyes.

Make sure you have a collar and leash on your dog at all times, especially when traveling.

truck unless he is securely tied on a very short lead. I've seen trucks stop quickly and, even though the dog was tied, it fell out and was dragged.

Another advantage of the crate is that it is a safe place to leave him if you need to run into the store. Otherwise you wouldn't be able to leave the windows down. Keep in mind that while many dogs are overly protective in their crates, this may not be enough to deter dognappers. In some states it is against the law to leave a dog in the car unattended.

Never leave a dog loose in the car wearing a collar and leash. More than one dog has killed himself by hanging. Do not let him put his head out an open window. Foreign debris can be blown into his eyes. When leaving your dog unattended in a car, consider the temperature. It can take less than five minutes to reach temperatures over 100 degrees Fahrenheit.

TRIPS

Perhaps you are taking a trip. Give consideration to what is best for your dog—traveling with you or boarding. When traveling by car, van or motor home, you need to think ahead about locking your vehicle. In all probability you have many valuables in the car and do not wish to leave it unlocked. Perhaps most valuable and not replaceable is your dog. Give thought to securing your vehicle and providing adequate ventilation for him. Another consideration for you when traveling with your dog is medical problems that may arise and little inconveniences, such as exposure to external parasites. Some areas of the country are quite flea infested. You may want to carry flea spray with you. This is even a good idea when staying in motels. Quite possibly you are not the only occupant of the room.

Unbelievably many motels and even hotels do allow canine guests, even some very first-class ones. Gaines Pet Foods Corporation publishes *Touring With Towser*, a directory of domestic hotels and motels that accommodate guests with dogs. Their address is Gaines TWT, PO Box 5700, Kankakee, IL, 60902. Call ahead to any motel that you may be considering and see if they accept pets. Sometimes it is necessary to pay a deposit against room damage. The management may feel reassured if you mention that your dog will be crated. If you do travel with your dog, take along plenty of baggies so that you can clean up after him. When we all do our share in cleaning up, we make it possible for motels to continue accepting our pets. As a matter of fact, you should practice cleaning up everywhere you take your dog.

Some pet clinics have technicians that pet sit and technicians that board clinic patients in their homes. This may be an alternative for you. Ask your veterinarian if they have an employee that can help you. There is a definite advantage of having a technician care for your dog, especially if your dog is on medication or is a senior citizen.

You can write for a copy of *Traveling With Your Pet* from ASPCA, Education Department, 441 E. 92nd Street, New York, NY 10128.

Depending on where your are traveling, you may need an up-to-date health certificate issued by your veterinarian. It is good policy to take along your dog's medical information, which would include the name, address and phone number of your veterinarian, vaccination record, rabies certificate, and any medication he is taking.

"Rascal" is another Lindemoen-trained Bulldog that shared the spotlight with some of Hollywood's best. Here he is pictured with co-star David Neidorf on the set of "Cover Up."

"Buford" takes a lunch break on the set of "The Rockateer." Always be certain to stick to your Bulldog's feeding schedule when away from home.

As a part of your family, your Bulldog will want to go everywhere with you.

AIR TRAVEL

When traveling by air, you need to contact the airlines to check their policy. Usually you have to make arrangements up to a couple of weeks in advance for traveling with your dog. The airlines require your dog to travel in an airline approved fiberglass crate. Usually these can be purchased through the airlines but they are also readily available in most pet-supply stores. If your dog is not accustomed to a crate, then it is a good idea to get him acclimated to it before your trip. The day of the actual trip you should withhold water about one hour ahead of departure and no food for about 12 hours. The airlines generally have temperature restrictions, which do not allow pets to travel if it is either too cold or too hot. Frequently these restrictions are based on the temperatures at the departure and arrival airports. It's best to inquire about a health certificate. These usually need to be issued within ten days of departure. You should arrange for non-stop, direct flights and if a commuter plane should be involved, check to see if it will carry dogs. Some don't. The Humane Society of the United States has put together a tip sheet for airline traveling. You can receive a copy by sending a self-addressed stamped envelope to:

The Humane Society of the United States
Tip Sheet
2100 L Street NW
Washington, DC 20037.

Regulations differ for traveling outside of the country and are sometimes changed without notice. Well in advance you need to write or call the appropriate consulate or agricultural department for instructions. Some countries have lengthy quarantines (six months), and countries differ in their rabies vaccination requirements. For instance, it may have to be given at least 30 days ahead of your departure.

Do make sure your dog is wearing proper identification including your name, phone number and city. You never know when you might be in an accident and separated from your dog. Or your dog could be frightened and somehow manage to escape and run away.

Another suggestion would be to carry in-case-of-emergency instructions. These would include the address and phone number of a relative or friend, your veterinarian's name, address and phone number, and your dog's medical information.

BOARDING KENNELS

Perhaps you have decided that you need to board your dog. Your veterinarian can recommend a good boarding facility or possibly a pet sitter that will come to your house. It is customary for the boarding kennel to ask for proof of vaccination for the DHLPP, rabies and bordetella vaccine. The bordetella should have been given within six months of boarding. This is for your protection. If they do not ask for this proof I would not board at their kennel. Ask about flea control. Those dogs that suffer flea-bite allergy can get in trouble at a boarding kennel. Unfortunately boarding kennels are limited on how much they are able to do.

For more information on pet sitting, contact NAPPS:

National Association of Professional Pet Sitters
1200 G Street, NW
Suite 760
Washington, DC 20005.

RESOURCES

Bulldog Club of America
Secretary, Ray Knudson
4300 Town Road
Salem, WI 53168
262-537-2771
bulldog@wi.net

Breeder Contact, Susan Rodenski,
P.O. Box 128
Sealston, Virginia 22547
540-775-3015
breedref@thebca.org

Rescue:
Bulldog Club of America
George Cromer
248-945-8009 or 800-594-4289, Michigan

American Kennel Club
260 Madison Avenue
New York, New York 10016
or 5580 Centerview Drive
Raleigh, North Carolina 27606
919-233-3600
919-233-9767
www.akc.org

The Kennel Club
1 Clarges Street
Picadilly, London W1Y 8AB, England

Canadian Kennel Club
100-89 Skyway Avenue
Etobicoke, Ontarion, Canada M9W6R4

INDEX

Adolescence, 54
Aggression, 119
Agility, 107
Air travel, 69, 157
Alcock, Sheila, Mrs., 14
American Kennel Club, 36, 96, 109
Balance, 48
Bandogs, 9
Barking, 122
Bathing, 72
Beamish, Captain W. R., 15
Biting, 125
Boarding kennels, 158
Body language, 116
Bordetella, 130
Breeders, 38
Brushing, 75
Bullbaiting, 10
Bulldog Club of America, 15
Bulldog Walk, 13
Bulldoggers, 16
Canadian Kennel Club, 96
Canine Good Citizen, 95, 106
Car travel, 67, 154
Character, 24
Chewing, 70, 143
Cheyletiella, 138
Coccidiosis, 134
Come command, 86
Conformation, 98-105
Coronavirus, 131
Crates, 79, 153
Dalziel, Hugh, 11
Demodectic mange, 138
Diet sheet, 51
Diet, 60, 64
—special, 64
Distemper, 129
Dockleaf, 13
Dog World, 14
Donald, 14
Down command, 90
Exercise, 69
Fear, 118
Feeding, 58

Fiennes, Richard and Alice, 7
Fighting, 26
Fleas, 135
Gender, 43
Giardiasis, 134
Grooming, 72
Head, 37
Health guarantee, 53
Health record, 49, 50
Heartworm disease, 135
Heat, 65
Heel command, 91
Hepatitis, 129
Hookworms, 132
Housetraining, 79
Humane Society of the United States, The, 158
Illness, 72
Immunizations, 128
Injury, 72
Inoculation record, 50
Jumping up, 123
Kendall, H. D., 14
Kennel Club, The, 96
Kennel cough, 130
King Dick, 12
King Orry, 13
Kippax Fearnought, Ch., 15
Lampier, Jacob, 12
Leash training, 85
Leptospirosis, 130
Lyme disease, 132
Mange, 138, 139
Microchipping, 148
Movement, 37
Nail care, 73
National Association of Professional Pet Sitters, 158
Natural History of Dogs, The, 7
Neutering, 44, 139
No command, 83
Nutrition, 58
Obedience, 93, 106
Panting, 67
Parasites, 132, 135
Parvovirus, 130

Pedigree, 50
Periodontal disease, 145
Philo-Kuan Standard, 12
Pools, 22
Puppy kindergarten, 82, 97
Puppy, 16, 38, 41, 42, 46, 47, 48
—health, 41, 42
—selection, 38
—show prospects, 46, 47
Rabies, 130
Registration certificate, 50
Robinson Crusoe, 14
Rosa, 12
Roundworms, 133
Sangster, Harry, 15
Sarcoptic mange, 138
Saylor, Dr. John A., 15
Sheffield Crib, Ch., 12
Sit command, 87
Skin problems, 56, 61, 75
Socialization, 53, 72, 114
Spaying, 44, 139
Stay command, 87
Stewart, Alex H., 15
Strathtay, Prince Albert, 15
Supplementation, 62
Tapeworms, 135
Tattooing, 148
Temperament, 48, 53
Therapy dog, 95
Ticks, 135
Toys, 70
Tracking, 107
Training classes, 93
Type, 48
Van Court, Albert E., 15
Verelst, H., 12
Verner, Sir William, 14
Veterinarian, 72, 144
—annual visit, 132
—first checkup, 126
—physical exam, 127
Westminster Kennel Club, 15
Whipworms, 133